1	Imprint Lanzarote... in a different way!	4
2	General map of places and places	5
3	Introduction travel	6
4	The abridg	9
4.1	La Gr	9
4.2	Mirad	9
4.3	Haría	9
4.4	Arrieta	10
4.5	Guatiza	10
4.6	Teguise	10
4.7	Tahíche	11
4.8	San Bartolomé	11
4.9	Arrecife	11
4.10	Puerto del Carmen	12
4.11	Puerto Calero	12
4.12	Montañas del Fuego	13
4.13	Yaiza	13
4.14	Femés	13
4.15	Playa Blanca	14
5	The visitor centres - Centros de Arte, Cultura y Turismo	14
5.1	Mirador del Río	16
5.2	Jameos del Agua	17
5.3	Las Cuevas de Los Verdes	20
5.4	Cactus Garden - Jardín de Cactus	22
5.5	House/ Museum César Manrique- Casa/ Museo César Manrique	23
5.6	Castillo San José- International Museum of Contemporary Art	25
5.7	Foundation César Manrique- Fundación César Manrique	26
5.8	Lagomar- Casa Omar Sharif	30
5.9	Pirate Museum in the Castillo de Santa Barbara - Museo de la Pirateria	31
5.10	Monumento al Campesino - The farm monument	32
5.11	Casa Amarilla - Arrecife	34
6	La Graciosa- The little pearl off Lanzarote	34
6.1	La Graciosa- The complete island tour	36
7	Vineyard La Geria	37
8	The Fire Mountains	38
8.1	Pilgrimage Church Ermita de Los Dolores	38

- 8.2 Timanfaya Visitor Centre- Centro de Visitantes 39
- 8.3 Timanfaya Fire Mountains - Montañas del Fuego 40
- 8.4 Isle of Hilario- Islote de Hilario 42
- 8.5 Timanfaya- Volcano route- La Ruta de los Volcanes 42
- 8.6 Timanfaya- Restaurant El Diablo 43
- 8.7 Timanfaya National Park - on your own or organized? 44
- 8.8 Camel Ride - Echadero de los Camellos 45
- 9 Lago Verde- Laguna de los Clicos 45
- 10 Los Hervideros 46
- 11 Saltworks of Janubio- Las Salinas de Janubio .. 47
- 12 Lanzarote- Fuerteventura 48
- 13 César Manrique- a unique artist 50
- 14 The Great César Manrique Tour 53
- 15 Beaches- Las Playas 53
- 16 Shopping - Shopping 58
  - 16.1 Tobacco products- Cigarettes 60
  - 16.2 Perfumeries- Profumerías 60
  - 16.3 Pharmacy- Farmacia 60
  - 16.4 Food 60
  - 16.5 Vvalue added tax 60
  - 16.6 Marina Lanzarote 61
- 17 Overview Markets- Mecados- Mercadillos 61
  - 17.1 Teguise Market - Mercadillo Teguise 62
  - 17.2 Arts and crafts market in Haría 63
- 18 Gastronomy 63
  - 18.1 Products 64
  - 18.2 Fishing 65
  - 18.3 Traditional dishes 65
- 19 Tapas- the little delicacies 65
  - 19.1 Restaurant recommendation Casa Félix- La Aulaga 66
  - 19.2 Restaurant recommendation Restaurante Monumento al Campesino 66
  - 19.3 Restaurant recommendation Bar Stop 66
  - 19.4 Restaurant recommendation El Diablo- Timanfaya 67
- 20 Gastronomy Events 67

- 20.1 Canary Island Day - The capital celebrates its independence...67
- 20.2 Festival Enogastronómico in Teguise.......68
- 21 museums 69
  - 21.1 Museum Tanit- Museo Tanit....................69
  - 21.2 House of Timple- Casa Del Timple 70
  - 21.3 Museum of sacred art in Haría- Museo de Arte Sacro 70
  - 21.4 Open Air Museum El Patio- Museo Agrícola El Patio 71
  - 21.5 Aviation Museum- Museo Aeronautico 72
  - 21.6 Wine Museum El Grifo- Museo El Grifo.....74
  - 21.7 Museum of History in Arrecife- Museo de Historia de Arrecife 75
  - 21.8 Cochineal Museum 75
- 22 Unique island artists 76
  - 22.1 The last basket weaver of Haría 76
  - 22.2 Autentica Ceramica Canaria in Haría 76
  - 22.3 The German potter Birgit Groth..............77
  - 22.4 The Jolateros - boats and souvenirs made of recycled sheet metal...79
- 23 Selected Discovery Tours...............................80
  - 23.1 Fascinating viewpoints 80
  - 23.2 The Northwest 81
  - 23.3 The contrasting north 82
  - 23.4 The volcanic fiery center 82
  - 23.5 The south coast 83
  - 23.6 Hike Montaña Colorada 83
  - 23.7 Hike Montaña del Cuervo 84
  - 23.8 Volcano Monte Corona - view into the crater 85
  - 23.9 Tramelan Hike - The Hike through the National Park 85
- 24 Cheese dairies- Queserías...............................87
  - 24.1 Cheese dairy El Faro..............................87
  - 24.2 Rubicón Cheese Dairy 88
- 25 Bodega Los Almacenes/ Mama Trina 88
- 26 German Bakery Andy Bread - Panadería Andy Bread 89
- 27 Aloe vera..90
- 28 Aquarium- Costa Teguise................................90
- 29 Aquapark Costa Teguise 91

30	Aqualava Playa Blanca	91
31	Hop On- Hop Off Arrecife	92
32	Boat trip Puerto del Carmen - Puerto Calero	92
33	Pardelas Park- Pardelas Restaurant	93
34	Rancho Texas Park	94
35	Bodega La Querencia	95
36	Telamon- The Titanic of Las Caletas Bay	96
37	Rental car	97
38	Anti- Boredom Activities	97
39	Lanzarote with children	98

1 Imprint Lanzarote... in a different way!

By Andrea Müller

The content of this e-book has been compiled with the greatest care. Nevertheless, errors cannot be completely excluded. The author assumes no legal responsibility or any liability for any remaining errors and their consequences. All trade names are used without warranty of merchantability and may be registered trademarks. All (also personal) illustrations were explicitly permitted only for this travel guide. A further use / passing on is expressly not permitted. The work including all its parts is protected by copyright. Any use - even in extracts - is only permitted with the consent of the author. All rights reserved.

Comments and questions are welcome:
Andrea Müller
Calle Las Cuevas, 91 - A2
E- 35542 Punta Mujeres, province of Las Palmas, Lanzarote
Web: www.lanzarote-mal-anders.de
mailto:ebook@lanzarote-mal-anders.de

© 2019 by Andrea Müller, cover design: Andrea Müller
Number of pages Printing variant: 98 pages
Number of images: 1 image

2   General map of places and places of interest

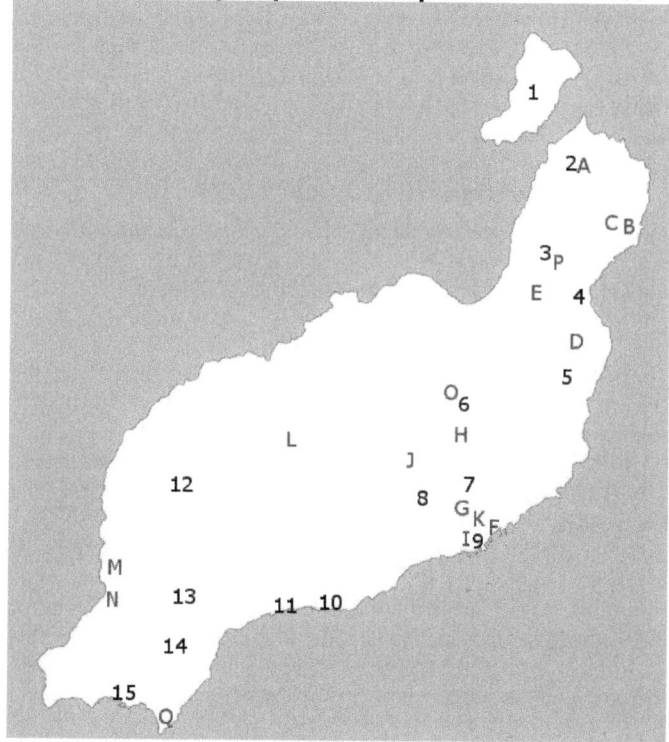

1= La Graciosa, **2**= Mirador del Rio, **3**= Haria, **4**= Arrieta, **5**= Guatiza, **6**= Teguise, **7**= Tahiche, **8**= San Bartolomé, **9**= Arrecife, **10**= Puerto del Carmen, **11**= Puerto Calero, **12**= Montañas del Fuego, **13**= Yaiza, **14**= Femés, **15**= Playa Blanca.

A= Mirador del Río, **B**= Jameos del Agua, **C**= Las Cuevas de Los Verdes, **D**= Kakteengarten- Jardín de Cactus, **E**= Haus/ Museum César Manrique- Casa/ Museo César Manrique, **F**= Castillo San José- Internationales Museum für zeitgenössische Kunst, **G**= Stiftung César Manrique- Fundación César Manrique, **H**= Lagomar- Casa Omar Sharif, **I**= Piratenmuseum im Castillo de Santa Barbara - Museo de la Pirateria, **J**= Bauerndenkmal- Monumento al Campesino, **K**= Casa

Amarilla - Arrecife, **L=** Wallfahrtskirche Ermita de Los Dolores,
M= Los Hervideros, **N=** Saltworks of Janubio- Las Salinas de Janubio, **O=** Teguise Market - Mercadillo Teguise, **P=** Handicraft Market in Haría, **Q=** Papagayo Beaches

3   Introduction travel guide Lanzarote

Lanzarote is the smallest of the Eastern Canary Islands and captivates with 300 volcanoes, which are embedded in a uniquely fascinating, contrasting landscape.

The evergreen, rugged and almost untouched north meets a sandy island center, which in the south changes into a volcanic moon and crater landscape with fire mountains.
To protect the natural beauty of the volcanic island and its cultural heritage, Lanzarote was declared a **Biosphere Reserve** by UNESCO on 07.10.1993.
Thanks to the important island artist **César Manrique,** Lanzarote was almost spared the serious building sins that took place on the neighbouring islands of Tenerife and Gran Canaria in the 1960s and 1970s. Benefit from his unique commitment to discover the many small white villages and be impressed by his unique work.

Enjoy in the north the indescribably beautiful view from the **Mirador del Río to** the small picturesque island **La Graciosa**.

In the lava tunnel of the **Cuevas de los Verdes** you explore the flaming, cooled heart of the earth.

and discover in the underground lake in **Jameos del Agua the** unique small, white albino crabs.

Drive to **Haría** in the valley of 1000 palm trees to stroll through the authentic **handicraft market**, visit the artist of authentic Canarian ceramics, or watch the last basket weaver of the island at work. Don't miss to visit the **Casa Museo César Manrique, the** last house of the unique island artist.

In the picturesque village of **Guatiza,** marvel at the grandiose variety of cacti in the cactus garden, the **Jardín de Cactus**.

Stroll through the small alleys of the former island capital **Teguise**, plunge into the grandiose hustle and bustle of the **Mercadillo de Teguise**, the largest weekly market on the island, or look over the entire island from the **Castillo Santa Barbara** with the Pirate Museum, the **Museo de la Piratería.**

In the **Museum Lagomar**, the house of Omar Sharif, experience architecture like in a fairy tale from 1001 nights and let yourself be fascinated by the **Fundación César Manrique**, the house with the underground lava bubbles.

Contemporary art can be seen in the ancient **Castillo San José** with the **Museo Internacional de Arte Contemporaneo**.

Immerse yourself in the hustle and bustle of the island capital **Arrecife**, stroll along the main shopping street **Calle Castillo y Léon**, enjoy the breathtaking view from the 17th floor of the **Gran Hotel Arrecife at a** café, or stroll around the **Charco de San Ginés** with its countless small fishing boats.

Explore the past in the Airport Museum, the **Aéronautico Museum, the** Agricultural Museum, the **El Patio Agrícola Museum**, the Ethnological Museum, the **Tanit Etnográfico Museum,** or the Wine Museum, the **El Grifo Vino Museum**.

In the geographical centre of the island, with the **Casa Museo Monumento al Campesino** and the striking **fertility statue,** you can enjoy **tapas** typical of the island after a tour.
Cross the unique wine-growing region of **La Geria on the** wine route and taste the island wines in one of the many **bodegas**.

From **Mancha Blanca** with the **Ermita de Los Dolores, the** patron saint of the island, via the Visitor Centre, the **Centro de Visitantes**, where volcanic simulations are shown, you can make your way to the fire mountains, the **Montañas del Fuego**.

Let yourself be impressed by the incredible volcanic landscape during an impressive drive through the **Timanfaya** area, experience fire and water demonstrations up close and taste food from the lava grill, which is powered exclusively by geothermal energy, in the **restaurant El Diablo**.

On the **Ruta de Camellos** you swing on the back of camels with a caravan through the mountains of fire.

Transfer from **Playa Blanca** to the neighbouring island of **Fuerteventura in** just 30 minutes to feel the fascination of the snow-white Caribbean beaches with crystal-clear water.

Purchase handmade sea salt in the **Salinas de Janubio** and be impressed by the rugged west coast with its magnificent natural spectacle in **Los Hervideros**.

Climb the **Lago de los Clicos** with the emerald green lagoon and stop for a fish meal in the picturesque fishing village of **El Golfo**.

Taste the delicious **goat's cheese** in the cheese dairies, **homemade jams, mojosauces** and **wines of** Mama Trina, or spoil your skin with **Aloe Vera** products of the island. Top addresses will lead you specifically to **local cuisine**, **tapas** and **gastronomic events**.

Start with the rental car to **5 varied routes**: The great César Manrique Tour, with all the highlights of the island artist, the contrasting north, the northwest, the volcanic fiery center and the south.

On **4 selected hikes you will** experience pure nature: Circle the colourful **Montaña Colorada** and the dark **Montaña de Cuervo**. Look into the highest mountain of the north, the **Monte Corona** and hike on the **Tremesana tour** through the Timanfaya National Park.

Take a day trip to the island of **La Graciosa** and let your soul dangle in the small bays or on the long sandy beaches, the **Playas de Papagayo**.

4   The abridged version from north to south
4.1   La Graciosa
The five islands of Alegranza, Roque del Este, Roque del Oeste, Montaña Clara and La Graciosa belong to the Chinijo archipelago. **La Graciosa** is separated from Lanzarote by the 1.5 km wide El Río estuary and is the only permanently inhabited island.

The settlement Caleta del Sebo, which is also the island harbour, offers restaurants, shopping and accommodation. In the interior, the volcanoes Las Agujas with 266 m and Montaña del Mojón with 188 m rise. Playa de las Conchas, located at the foot of Montaña Bermeja at 157 m, is considered the most beautiful beach on the island. A ferry regularly crosses from Órzola to La Graciosa in 30 minutes.

4.2   Mirador del Río
The **Mirador del Río** is a vantage point located in the north of the island 475 m above the cliffs in a former military post. The building, designed by César Manrique, offers with its outdoor terraces and the view through the "eyes" a fantastic view of La Graciosa.

4.3   Haría
The municipality of **Haría** in the north of the island still lives from agriculture. Potatoes, onions, peas and wine are grown all around. The Mirador de Guinate offers beautiful views of the coastal landscape and the island of La Graciosa.

From the viewpoint Mirador de Haría, one has a fantastic view to the "**Valley of the Thousand Palms**", the biggest palm grove of the island. In the town centre there is the shady green avenue, León y Castillo, which leads to the church. Every Saturday there is a large handicraft market with exclusively homemade objects and products from the island. A little away from the centre are the last residence of César Manrique and the workshop of the last basket weaver of the island.

4.4 Arrieta
The former fishing village of **Arrieta,** situated on the east coast, and the neighbouring village of Punta Mujeres are characterised by whitewashed houses. The **Jameos del Agua** cave is part of a 6 km long lava tunnel that runs from the La Corona volcano to the sea and continues 1.5 km further under the seabed. Inside there is a lagoon in which a white, blind crab, unique in the world, lives. The **Cueva de los Verdes** belongs to the same part of the tunnel, a tunnel that is accessible on different levels.

4.5 Guatiza
The small village of **Guatiza** was the center of scale insect breeding on the island, growing prickly pears to make the red dye fireplace. In the meantime the village is experiencing a revival, characterized by the reforestation of the old cactus fields and the new museum where the history is presented. Worth seeing is the cactus garden designed by César Manrique, the **Jardín de Cactus**, with over 1400 cactus species. From the windmill above the cactus terraces you have a wonderful view over the whole complex.

4.6 Teguise
The historic town of **Teguise**, once a bishop's seat and administrative capital of the island until 1852, is still called La Villa, the town, by its inhabitants today. In the centre is the church of San Miguel with the Virgin of Guadelupe, restored at the beginning of the 20th century. In the church square there is the Zenthaus La Cilla, a former church granary from the 17th century and the Palacio Spinola with a timple exhibition. Every Sunday the largest market on the island, the **Mercadillo, takes** place here with over 500 stalls.

The former fortress, the **Castillo Santa Barbara** with a pirate museum, towers over the city on a volcanic mountain.

The municipality of Teguise includes the large holiday resort of **Costa Teguise, which** lies directly on the sea.

Worth seeing is the former estate of Omar Sharif, the **Lagomar** in Nazaret.

In the fertile valley of Los Valles, on a hill, is the church of **Ermita de las Nieves, from where** you can enjoy a fantastic view over the island to Fuerteventura.

At the 4 km long beach **Playa de Famara** windsurfers and kitesurfers get their money's worth.

4.7 Tahíche

The town of **Tahíche is called the** suburb of Lanzarote's capital Arrecife. In Taro de Tahíche there is the **Fundación César Manrique**, the house with the underground lava bubbles.

4.8 San Bartolomé

The small town of **San Bartolomé is** situated on the edge of the most important agricultural area of La Geria, between the villages of Tías and Uga, with the largest wine-growing area of Lanzarote.

In the geographical centre of the island there is a replica of a picturesque old farming village, the **Casa/ Museo del Campesino** with the **fertility statue** dedicated to the island's farmers.

The agricultural museum **El Patio** in Tiagua shows different types of mills as well as field and handicraft equipment.

The **Museo Etnografico Tanit**, the ethnographic museum, exhibits a collection of objects that have been collected on the island over almost 100 years.

4.9 Arrecife

The capital and port of **Arrecife is the** seat of the island government and was home to the largest fishing fleet in the Canary Islands.

The former disgrace of Arrecifes, a 17-storey skyscraper converted into the **Grand Hotel Arrecife**, is the most striking point of the island. From the café on the 17th floor you have a wonderful view over the city to Puerto del Carmen and Fuerteventura. In front of the hotel is the city beach, **Playa de Reducto,** which is a feast for the eyes at high tide.

A landmark of the city is the spherical bridge that connects the city center with the fortress, the **Castillo San Gabriel.** The large cannons in front of the entrance come from the former military post of the Mirador del Río. From here, the long shopping street, **Calle León y Castillo, invites you to go** shopping and visit the **Casa Amarilla** with its insular changing exhibitions.
Worth seeing is the church **San Ginés** with the figures of the patron saint of the city and the Madonna of the Rosary. At the adjacent picturesque **Charco de San Ginés,** one has a view from small restaurants to countless fishing boats.
On the northern outskirts of the city, the fortress, **Castillo San José** with drawbridge and moat, was converted under the direction of César Manrique into the **Museum of Contemporary Art, the Museo Internacional de Arte Contemporaneo MIAC.** Not far from here is the port of Puerto de los Mármoles, where the large cruise ships anchor.

4.10 Puerto del Carmen
The former harbour town **Puerto del Carmen** is Lanzarote's largest holiday area with the long beaches **Playa de Matagorda**, **Playa de los Pocillos**, **Playa Grande** and the beautiful view of Fuerteventura. An endless shopping mile with countless shopping possibilities, pubs and restaurants runs through the centre.

4.11 Puerto Calero
The chic, manageable marina **Puerto Calero** offers a selection of restaurants and boutiques. From here the Catlanza catamaran to the Papagayo beaches and the U-boat to dive into the Atlantic start among other things.

4.12 Montañas del Fuego

The national park **Timanfaya** in the fire mountains, the **Montañas del Fuego**, is the main attraction of Lanzarote.

At the **Islote de Hilario**, in front of the restaurant El Diabolo, the access road of the 50 sqkm large volcanic landscape ends. The place lies above a magma chamber, whose temperatures reach already 10 m under the earth over 600 degrees. A breathtaking ride through the volcanic landscape, as well as impressive demonstrations follow.

Not far from the access road to Timanfaya, at **Echadero de Camellos, there is** the possibility of a dromedary ride on the slope of the volcano.

The visitor's centre, the **Centro de Visitantes**, offers an exhibition and film screening on the theme of volcanoes. In addition, free guided hikes are offered, such as the **Tremesana hike** through the national park.

In **Mancha Blanca there is** the sanctuary of the **Ermita de Nuestra Señora de los Dolores,** dedicated to the patron saint of the island.

4.13 Yaiza

The small town of **Yaiza, which** has won first place in several beauty contests, is the centre of the district of the same name. Corpus Christi large coloured salt carpets are scattered on the forecourt of the church, in the Advent season a miniature replica of the island is erected.

There are 3 other attractions in the coastal area: the **Salinas de Janubio**, the natural spectacle of **Los Hervideros** and the fishing village of **El Golfo**.

4.14 Femés

The small village of **Femés is** situated on the edge of the protected Los Ajaches mountain range and is the shortest connection to Playa Blanca. At a height of 350 m, the forecourt of the church offers an indescribable view over Playa Blanca to Fuerteventura.

4.15 Playa Blanca

It was not until the mid-1980s that the tiny fishing village of **Playa Blanca became** the island's third largest holiday resort. Besides the artificially arranged main beaches, **Playa Flamingo** and **Playa Dorada**, the **Papagayo beaches** with their 7 different sized bays belong to the "non plus ultra".

The ferries to Fuerteventura leave every hour from the port of Playa Blanca. The snow-white dune landscape and the beaches of Corralejo are among the highlights of the neighbouring island.

5 The visitor centres - Centros de Arte, Cultura y Turismo

9 centres can be visited, of which 8 are chargeable and up to 6 can be purchased as combination **bono tickets at a** reduced price.

In the north of the island, on the Risco de Famara hill, is the **Mirador del Río** viewpoint, from which you can enjoy a fantastic view of the island of La Graciosa, which lies in front of the island, and in the **Cueva de los Verdes**, which leads through a long lava tunnel, you can explore the heart of the earth.

In the **Jameos del Agua** the worldwide unique small crab species can be observed and in the cactus garden **Jardín de Cactus** more than 1400 species are presented.

The free **Casa Monumento al Campesino** with the Museum House of the Farmer and the Statue of Fertility is located in the geographical centre of Lanzarote, from where access to any point on the island is possible.

Near Arrecife, in the old military fortress, the Castillo San José, there is the International Museum of Contemporary Art, the **Museo Internacional de Arte Contempráneo - MIAC** with modern works of art.

In the south, in the Timanfaya National Park, lie the **Montañas del Fuego** Fire Mountains, formed by volcanic eruptions between 1730 and 1736.

Different **BONO tickets**, combination tickets, are offered, with which up to 10.55 € can be saved. They are valid for 14 days. Children up to 6 years are free, from 7-12 years half price will be charged.

1st possibility: Bono 3 centers: price 21,00 €. Here you can choose from Jameos del Agua, Montañas del Fuego and the Cueva de los Verdes, 2 centers. Then one has to decide between the Mirador del Río and the Jardín del Cactus. The maximum saving compared to the single entrance fee is 4,30 €.

2nd possibility: Bono 4 centers: price 28,00 €. It contains the Jameos del Agua, the Cueva de los Verdes and the Montañas del Fuego. As the fourth centre, one can again decide between the Mirador del Río and the Jardín del Cactus. The maximum saving is 6,80 €.

3rd possibility: Bono 6 centers: price 33,00 €. With this ticket you can visit all centers and save 10,55 € per person.

Visiting hours: (Summer time: 1 July - 30 September)
Museo Internacional de Arte: all year 10.00 - 20.00 hrs.
Monumento al Campesino: 10.00 - 17.45 all year round
Jardín del Cactus: Summer: 9.00- 17.45, Winter: 10.00- 17.45 o'clock
Cueva de los Verdes: all year 10.00 - 19.00 h, last visit 18.00 h
Jameos des Agua: all year 10.00 - 18.30 o'clock
Mirador del Río: summer 10.00-18.45, winter: 10.00- 17.45 o'clock
Montañas del Fuego: Summer: 9.00- 18.45, last trip: 18.00, winter: 9.00- 17.45, last trip 17.00

BONO tickets are available on request at all cash desks in the centres.
The Casa Amarilla in Arrecife with temporary, island exhibitions and the **Museo Atlántico** underwater museum, for which a diving licence is required, cannot be combined with the Bono ticket.

5.1 Mirador del Río

In the extreme north, the **Mirador del Río,** at 475 m, is the highest viewpoint of Lanzarote, offering a magnificent view of the cliffs of the Famara mountain range and the offshore island of La Graciosa.

The building, designed by the island artist César Manrique, was completed in 1973 and captivates with its volcanic stone façade, which adapts to the surroundings like a camellion and is therefore not obviously perceived. The wrought-iron steel sculpture, a combination of fish and bird, decorates the entrance to the Mirador.

A meandering tunnel leads into two large vaults, in front of which are the large window facades, the so-called "eyes" of the vantage point.

The grandiose viewing platform, which protrudes into the deep abyss, can be reached through the side doors of the cafeteria.

Here, through the robust railing, the feeling creeps in of standing at a ship's railing and soon arriving at the picturesque neighbouring island of La Graciosa.

At the back of the cafeteria, the dynamically curved spiral staircase leads to the upper floors of the Mirador with a souvenir shop, a seating area overlooking **Monte Corona**, the highest volcano in the north, and another viewing platform overlooking La Graciosa.

On clear days, the view from the Mirador is a feast for the eyes, but in case of heavy clouds, apart from low clouds, absolutely nothing can be seen. In these cases only the architecture of the viewpoint can be admired.

To enjoy the almost identical view of La Graciosa, park your rental car at Mirador del Río and walk along the small road on the left before the viewpoint. Alternatively, turn left into this street and pass the coast. Small parking bays and wall breakthroughs on the land side offer holding possibilities, at which you can park the vehicle.

Nostalgia: For the 1979 ZDF Christmas series "**Tim Thaler, The Sold Laugh**", the shooting took place at Mirador del Río, the Baron's residence, among other places.

5.2 Jameos del Agua

The cave system **Jameos del Agua** lies in the north, at the LZ-1 direction Orzola and was formed by the eruptions of the volcano La Corona. The word Jameos comes from the vocabulary of the natives, the Guanches, and means earth opening or deepening in the earth. The overall concept of the complex was designed by César Manrique and opened in 1966.

After the entrance, a curved lava stone staircase leads down to the first level of Jameos, which ends in a restaurant.

In the rear part there is a bar area harmoniously set into the cave walls, next to which the illuminated tunnel line, which comes directly from the volcano La Corona, was set in scene.

Past lush green plants, the next curved staircase leads directly to the lake with the crabs.

It is a small white, blind crayfish that otherwise only occurs at depths of over 2,000 metres and grows to a maximum of 1.5 cm in height.

The water level of the lake sinks and rises with the tides, as the grotto is fed by sea water, which seeps through the rock, despite the lack of connection to the sea.

A narrow lava stone path for the rear part of the Jameos.

Although the lake appears deep, it is shallow as the high ceiling is impressively reflected on the water surface.

About in the middle of the lake you can see an opening in the vaulted ceiling through which daylight penetrates. This was caused by an explosion when the lava came into contact with the sea water, so that the penetrating rays of light are reflected on the surface of the water.

At the back of the lake you can see the fascinating reflections of the entrance side on the water surface. Once again, seating invites you to linger.
Upwards, stairs integrated into the vault on both sides lead to the next level with a bar and seating.

It is fascinating how many different levels the light reflections in the lake and the thick lava rock can be perceived from. Further stairs lead to the next level to the outside area, on which stairs also open up a small green garden landscape.

Outside, next to the crabs, is the second fascinating attraction of the complex: a shrill, alpine white pool landscape with turquoise blue water interspersed with black monoliths forms an extreme contrast to the dark boulders and transforms the site into an oasis inviting to a photo shoot. The oblique high palm tree reflected in the pool makes all shots the perfect photo motif.
On the left side downstairs, also the fancy bar creation with thick black lava stones, which serve as the seat of the bar stools, should be suitable for the perfect photo.

To the left of the pool, the path leads to the **auditorium of** the complex.
The auditorium with 600 seats in 19 ascending rows is located in an impressive volcanic tunnel, where regular events take place after repairs.

In the outdoor area, another spiral staircase leads to the starting level. From two large terraces with a bar one enjoys a fantastic view over the whole pool complex, to the sea and the Malpais de La Corona.

From the right terrace, one gets into the house of the volcanoes, the **Casa de los Volcanes**, in which there is an exhibition that was awarded in 2002, but that is meanwhile technically outdated.

Further on you reach the upper part of the exhibition.

Since mid-2018, a new permanent exhibition on **Jesús Soto Morales has been taking place** in these exhibition rooms, paying homage to the deceased "Master of Invisible Light".

He was born in Fuerteventura in 1928, came to Lanzarote at the age of 20, where he founded his own lighting company and worked independently until he was contracted by the island government, the Cabildo Lanzarote.

One of his first projects was the Castillo San Gabriel in Arrecife, which he skilfully staged with its outdoor lighting. Only 10 years later, in 1965, he became the technical and artistic director of the Cuevas de los Verdes and the Jameos del Agua. Initially Soto was only commissioned to install simple lighting for the archaeologists and speleologists, but he took the opportunity to perfectly illuminate the caves to show the fascination of the volcanic rock.

Jesús Soto combined fantasy, creativity, technical knowledge and absolute respect for the volcanic island in his works. When the Jameos del Agua was already under construction, Soto and his team ordered a partial dismantling, so that the stairs to the cave exit, the descent to the lagoon with the blind crabs and the adjacent path to the rear part of the cave was changed according to his ideas.

He also designed the Ruta de los Volcanes, the route through the Timanfaya National Park. In order to determine the most beautiful route through the volcanic mountains, he studied plans and aerial photographs, spent several days in the area and chose a route that had the minimum impact on nature and the maximum impact on visitors. For Soto, sustainability was the top priority in his projects.

His most brilliant move was to convince the island government to let **César Manrique** return to Lanzarote from New York. He said: "**I thought it was a necessary step for Lanzarote to be known in the art world and in international tourism**".

Soto also worked in El Golfo, the Mirador del Río, the Monumento al Campesino and the Cactus Garden, designed the square Simón Bolivar in Arrecife, the Lagomar in Nazaret, the altar of the church of San Ginés, the gardens of Hotel Beatriz, the church square of Iglesia Magdalena in Masdache, a discotheque in Playa Honda, several houses in Arrecife and Puerto del Carmen, a palace in Saudi Arabia and a fountain in Madrid.

Jesús Soto Morales was appointed in 2002 as the "adopted son of the island", the honorary citizen status for those not born on Lanzarote. On 04.05.2003 he died in Arrecife and was buried in the cemetery San Román.

The curved path that runs in front of the complex can be photographed again.

With a magnificent view of the coast, you can see the small white villages of Punta Mujeres and Arrieta, followed by Mala and Guatiza, where the cactus garden is located. The obligatory souvenir shop is at the exit.

By the way: All the tables and chairs in the complex come from an old stranded sailing ship, parts of which César Manrique has transformed into a wall sculpture in the exhibition.

5.3 Las Cuevas de Los Verdes

The cave system **Las Cuevas de Los Verdes is located** in the north of the island and is integrated into the wide volcanic landscape of the Malpais de la Corona.

When the volcano **La Corona** erupted more than 3000 years ago, a 6 km long underground volcanic tunnel was formed, which stretches from the volcanic cone to the sea. In this tunnel are the Cuevas de los Verdes and further down, just before the sea, the Jameos del Agua.

The visit of the cave is a journey into the flaming, cooled heart of the earth, spectacular and unique at the same time.

The approximately one kilometre long area that can be visited is made up of superimposed galleries with vertical connections that make it possible to see plains from different perspectives. You can see lava channels, solid blocks carried by the lava flow, lava drops, salt deposits and solidified lava layers. The vault and the walls appear in spectacular colours.

The tour inside the earth takes about 50 minutes. After the ticket has been purchased, groups of about 50 people are grouped together.
After a short briefing in Spanish and English, we quickly go out of a mix of upstairs, downstairs, straight ahead again, partly bent over, through the cave.

Inside there is a constant temperature of 20 degrees. At particularly interesting points, short explanations are given by the guide. Shortly before the end of the tour it gets really exciting and fascinating again. The guide points to a fabulously deep hole in the cave, with the announcement: No Pictures, no Pictures, children please stay behind, "take care", as the barrier consists of a balustrade that is not even knee-high. You can find out everything else on site.

Important: Be sure to wear sturdy shoes, flip-flops are unsuitable. There are no toilets in the entire complex. You will find the next places before the Cuevas de los Verdes on the side of the parking lot.

Background information: The interior of the caves began in 1960 and was completed in 1964. The lighting was created by Jésus Soto, one of César Manrique's closest collaborators. He also realized the Lagomar and defined the volcanic route through the Timanfaya area.

Worth knowing: Las Cuevas de los Verdes means translated the caves of the green. But they are not called so because they are in the green north of the island, but because the Verde family, translated as green, lived here at that time.
When Lanzarote suffered from pirate attacks in the 16th and 17th centuries, the cave's intricate galleries served as a hideout and refuge for the island's inhabitants.

5.4 Cactus Garden - Jardín de Cactus

The cactus garden, **Jardín de Cactus, is** located on the road between Guatiza and Mala. Already from a distance you can see a small windmill with a red roof, which serves as a signpost.
In front of the entrance, the oversized, 8 m high green steel cactus is enthroned as a landmark of the complex, which was designed by the island artist César Manrique.

In the past, Koschenillen were bred on cactus figs in the entire area between Guatiza and Mala. Coming from Mexico, Coschenille produces a carmine that has been used since the Aztecs for dyeing fabrics, food and cosmetics. In 1835 they arrived in Lanzarote. Cactus shoots were planted in spring and infected with insects if they were of sufficient size. In summer they were carefully harvested with tin spoons. The process of drying and cleaning to preserve the coschenille as a whole was meticulous and strictly traditional. Since the red dye was produced artificially, however, the breeding lost importance.

César Manrique used an abandoned volcanic pit to realize his idea of a large cactus garden. More than 10,000 plants can be admired, of which more than 1,000 belong to cacti species and thickleaf plants. The garden has the shape of an amphitheatre, with stepped beds that can be reached via paths paved with volcanic stones.
In the middle of the complex the beds are larger and decorated with huge monoliths. At the back there is a souvenir shop and a snack bar, where you can relax with a drink and feel the whole atmosphere.

The snack bar currently also offers a delicious selection of tapas: Papas arrugadas with mojo sauces, Spanish tortilla, stuffed olives with red mojo sauce, fresh goat cheese with olive oil, anchovies in garlic and coriander, Canarian fish salad with octopus, marinated tuna, eagle fish cubes with papas arrugadas, meatballs, ham and fish croquettes.

Tip: If you are not yet familiar with the typical Canarian shriveled potatoes, the Papas arrugadas, you can try them here.

5.5 House/ Museum César Manrique- Casa/ Museo César Manrique

The **Casa/ Museo César Manrique** was the last residence of the important artist César Manrique. It is located in Haría and is indicated on all road signs in the village.

In 1987, the artist gave up his former residence in Tahíche, the seat of today's Fundación César Manrique, and moved to his new home in Haría. He built it on the ruins of an old historic house belonging to the village doctor Paco Fierro and lived there until his tragic accidental death.

The 12,000 square metre property is littered with large, thick old palm trees. The house is on the right, front part, the artist's large studio is separately on the back part of the site.

Small, black lava stones, which are spread all over the property, lead to the entrance. One enters a small inner courtyard, the Zitronenhof, on the left side there is the cash register. There you will receive a plan containing additional information about the rooms of the house. Unfortunately no photos may be taken in the house, only outdoor shots and photos in the studio are allowed. The tour starts on the right side.

First you reach the gallery courtyard, which was designed by Manrique with traditional old utensils. On the right-hand side, on the upper floor, there is a picturesque, traditionally crafted wooden lattice balcony.

When you enter the building, you are standing in the dressing room for guests, with adjoining bathroom.

From the inner courtyard of the house you enter the hallway on the left side. A heavy, dark wooden ceiling and a terracotta floor decorated with stars recall the traditional architecture of the island.

On the left side there is a bedroom and a bathroom. Through the original arrangement of the artist's utensils, the feeling constantly arises that César Manrique could walk back in the door at any moment.
In the spacious bathroom, the interior and exterior space form a harmonious unit through a light glass porch; countless cosmetic items on the shelf above the washbasin complete the overall picture.

Through the bedroom back, past the hallway, you reach the living room, the largest and most central room of the house. Here a small bathroom, a kitchen and a dining room are attached.
The small bathroom on the inside looks as bright as day due to the surrounding mirrors and circular recesses in the ceiling.

The adjacent kitchen is country style, has a hatch to the living room and has an exit to a covered pergola.
The open living room, overlooking the exterior, is dominated by a basalt fireplace decorated with earthenware vessels. In front of it there is a comfortable seating area, next to it on the frame of an old sewing machine substructure, a filled liquor bar.
On the right side of the seating group there is a black wing with countless photographs.

In the adjoining dining room with a long dining table, the first meeting was held in which the creation of the César Manrique Foundation was decided.

Outside, in front of the pool, another bedroom and bathroom area adjoins the building.
Behind the pool there are two seating groups and loungers, which are covered by a pergola.
Finally, it is possible to watch a film about the artist on a flat screen outside next to the dining room. You can also find the report on YouTube: Taro, El eco de César Manrique.
The further way leads to the studio, which is located at the back of the property.

This is where César Manrique retired every day to work. The workshop is littered with tables full of drawings, easels, cans of acrylic lacquer and various objects. Everything was preserved as the artist had left it before his death in 1992.

5.6 Castillo San José- International Museum of Contemporary Art

The International Museum of **Contemporary** Art, the **Museo Internacional de Arte Contemporáneo MIAC, is located in the** San José Castle, which served as a military fortress. It was built in the 18th century during the reign of the Bourbon Carlos III.

On the initiative of César Manrique, the dilapidated building was converted into a museum and opened in 1975. The artist personally led the reconstruction work and the development, but hardly changed the internal structure of the castle. In the outbuildings, Manrique designed a restaurant that represents the most striking intervention in the architecture of the old fortress.

Payment is made in the container on the left side of the castle.

Access to the building is via the old drawbridge. Impressive are the thick vaulted walls, with temporary art exhibitions.

If you follow the stairs up to the upper floor, you can see from the industrial harbour, the Muelle de Los Mármoles, up to the highest building of the city, the Gran Hotel Arrecife.

The restaurant **QUÉ MUAC is located** in the basement, which can be reached via a curved staircase.

From the restaurant upstairs through another gallery you get back to the entrance area.
TIP: You can reach the **QUÉ MUAC restaurant** without visiting the museum via the outside staircase, which leads down to the left of the museum.

5.7 Foundation César Manrique- Fundación César Manrique

The **Fundación César Manrique** was founded in 1982 by the island artist with a group of his closest friends and officially inaugurated in 1992.

It is a private cultural foundation which is self-financing, non-profit-making and promotes artistic activity in a natural and cultural environment.

The property with its farm buildings and garages was personally redesigned by César Manrique in order to use it as a museum within the framework of his foundation.

The complex is located on a 30,000 sq.m. plot of land, which is traversed by deep black lava flows, which were created during strong volcanic eruptions in the years 1730 to 1736.

The building was built on five large underground lava bubbles. The pure living space amounts to 1,800 square meters, to which still 1,200 square meters of terraces and gardens belong.

The upper floor is rather simple, in the style of Lanzarote's traditional architecture, but on closer inspection one notices that Manrique has fully integrated nature into the house. The basement is pure fascination. Five large lava bubbles were connected by small cave passages through basalt passages and made habitable. In the green outdoor area there is a recreation area with pool, dance floor, sitting area and barbecue. In the last part of the house you will find the artist's large studio.

Following a detailed description: The signposted Fundación is located at LZ-1 in Tahiche. Already on the parking lot there is a big white wind chime on the left side. It bears the name La Energía de la Pirámida, the energy of the pyramid. The view reaches from here to the Gran Hotel Arrecife and to the white dunes of Corralejo in Fuerteventura.

Continue through the Manrique-designed entrance gate to the pay house, which is on the left.

Passing a lava stone field with semicircular lava walls, as in the wine-growing area La Gería, following a colourful wind chime on the right side and an eroded sculpture, one approaches the entrance.
On the entrance door, made of dark solid wood, hangs a small door sign in the form of a key with the inscription Manrique. Now one enters the small inner courtyard, where the upper openings of two lava bubbles are visible on the right side. The branches of a palm tree protrude from one of these openings. The walls are decorated with white bones and objects.

Continue to the left, directly into the light-flooded living room with adjoining kitchen, in which there is a small picture exhibition. Apart from the direct, fantastic view of the lava flows with the volcanoes behind them, the circular railings in the living room are immediately noticeable. Here there is a direct connection to the underlying volcanic bubbles. The larger one, from which a tree rises, was according to the story, the bubble that Manrique was the first to discover in the black lava field. On closer inspection, he discovered that a fig tree grew out of a lava bubble.

From the balustrade behind, a narrow spiral staircase, which is unfortunately not accessible, leads directly into the volcano bubble, which is located under the living room.
The tour continues, past a mirror wall, to the outside. From here, one has a view over the black lava fields to the snow-white beaches of Fuerteventura.

On the way to the next showroom, you can see the green pool area of the house on the lower left.
Arriving in the building, the room opens a wide view of the fascinating lava landscape through its large window front.

Here is a documentation of César Manrique's works: the Mirador del Rio, the Jameos del Agua, the Restaurant El Diablo in the Timanfaya National Park, the Jardín de Cactus and the Museo Internacional de Arte

Contemporáneo. The exhibition also includes views of a design of the cemetery portal with garden in Cadiz, a floor plan of the Mirador del Río and the Mirador El Palmarejo on La Gomera, and watercolour drawings.

Auf der rechten Seite des Raumes ist eine Tafel mit seinen berühmtesten Werken angebracht: 1968- Jameos del Agua in Haría, 1968- Taro de Tahíche in Teguise, 1969- Casa del Campesino in San Bartolomé, 1970- Restaurante El Diabolo im Nationalpark Timanfaya, 1971- Complejo Costa Martíanez in Puerto de la Cruz auf Teneriffa, 1973- Mirador del Río in Haría, 1974- Castillo San José in Arrecife, 1977- Auditorio De Los Jameos Del Agua in Haría, 1982- La Vaguada in Madrid, 1989 Mirador de La Peña in Valverde auf der Insel El Hierro, 1990- Jardín del Cactús in Teguise, 1991- Jardín de Palmajero in Valle Gran Rey auf La Gomera und 1992- Playa Jardín in Puerto de la Cruz auf Teneriffa.

From the hallway, with white floors and walls, a lava basin embedded in the wall, above which there is a green fern, you enter the living room of the property.
Here there is a frontal chimney made of lava stones and to the right of it the wedel staircase which leads to the basement to the lava bubbles.
Two steps lead to the next two rooms. In the first one a wall-sized mirror on the left side immediately stands out. In two corners the tile mirror does not go through to the wall. Here plants were embedded in volcanic ash, so that one has the feeling that the plants would grow out of the floor. Again the "green corners" are accentuated by ferns suspended from the ceiling.
The second room shows an exhibition with sketches of the artist's designs, drawings, small sculptures and clay works.
To the right, a lava staircase planted on the sides leads to the basement and the volcanic bubbles.

In the first bubble you pass a small black pebble fountain and go through the first basalt passage into the second bubble. There is a white settee along the wall with a marble table and a palm tree.

Fascinating is that the palm protrudes from the open bubble. One encounters a harmonious combination of different colours and lava layers.

In the next bubble, three red seating groups were arranged. Now you are directly under the living room. In the middle is the tree Manrique had seen on the lava field. At the back of the bubble, the narrow spiral staircase leads up to the living room.

Past a bathroom we continue to the inner courtyard, which is also of volcanic origin and lushly planted with palm trees and cacti. Here you will find a seating area hidden in the rock, a barbecue area and a small snow-white pool with turquoise blue water.

Now you leave the green oasis through a basalt passage and enter the fourth bubble, which is supported by 4 corner pillars. The passage leads down into the last bubble. Here again a tree is arranged in the middle, the top of which protrudes from the bubble opening. The seating groups and the luminaires are yellow-white chequered. Again, plants with volcanic stones were embedded in the white soil.

From the last bubble we go directly to the large, former Atelier Manrique, where a permanent exhibition of the artist is presented.

On the left side a large lava rock protrudes into the room, which is only separated from the outside by a gas disc.

One has the feeling of standing directly in a lava field. In all other rooms a thick lava boulder protrudes from each corner.

If you leave the studio, you can see a bathroom on the right, almost covered by plants. Upstairs the toilets are on the left side.

The path continues into a large courtyard with a small black pond. In the middle the water splashes from a lava boulder. A long, large, colorful mural by the artist adorns the left wall. Small volcanic stones were used for the contours and pieces of tiles for the interior surfaces.

After this on the left side, in the former garages, there is a snack bar, followed by a souvenir shop. The adjoining, roofed seating invites you to linger for a while.

5.8 Lagomar- Casa Omar Sharif

The former house of Omar Sharif, or as it is called today the **Lagomar**, is situated directly in and in front of a volcano, which is located above the village Nazaret. Take the LZ-10 in the direction of Teguise, turn off at the MUSEO sign and follow the road to the "broken off mountain".

On the slope of the volcano, in an old quarry, this unique property was designed by César Manrique in the 1970s and realized by Jésus Soto. The artists created a fairy tale like from 1000 and one night.

The legend: When the actor **Omar Sharif** visited the house during his shooting of the movie "Herrscher einer versunkenen Welt" he was so overwhelmed by its fascination that he immediately decided to buy it. However, after the infamous bridge game in which he had lost the house, it fell into the hands of various owners.

It is said that a real estate agent knew about Sharif's passionate bridge playing and asked him to play a game. Without knowing that his opponent were European champions, Sharif put his newly-acquired house on the line to win the game in the belief. He lost and left his house, which he had owned only one day, and never returned to Lanzarote. Since then the estate has been known as **Casa Omar Sharif.**

In 1984 the German architect Dominik Böttinger travelled to the Canary Islands and felt attracted by the magic of the house when he arrived in Lanzarote. After five years he was the new owner of the property and returned to the island with his wife to tackle the final phase of the Lagomar.

Captivated by the uniqueness of this place, the couple decided to make it accessible to the public. In addition, a restaurant was to be built in part of the quarry. They had the vision of creating a space that would delight all the senses and host art exhibitions, gastronomy and concerts.

Once again, it was César Manrique who advised the architectural couple so that the Lagomar could be opened in 1997.

TIP: The visit of the property is absolutely recommendable and forms a symbiosis of all worth seeing objects, which Manrique and Soto realized on the island. Another highlight is the white tube tunnel through which you can walk on wooden steps over the water.

As the property is elevated in the quarry, one enjoys a fantastic view to Arrecife, which is the highest building of the Grand Hotel. After the tour you will understand why Omar Sharif fell in love with the property.

5.9 Pirate Museum in the Castillo de Santa Barbara - Museo de la Pirateria

The Pirate Museum is located in the castle, the **Castillo de Santa Barbara**, in Teguise. If one approaches the old island capital, one discovers the Castillo above the city on a volcanic mountain.

You drive up the winding road to the castle and have the possibility to park your car directly in front of the entrance. From there one enjoys a wonderful view over Teguise. On a clear day you can see Costa Teguise, Arrecife, Fuerteventura and the Fire Mountains all the way to the island of Graciosa.

In order to protect the island population from pirate attacks, a fortress was built in the 16th century on the remains of a small fort from the 14th century.

However, the siege of pirates caused so much damage to the fortress that the Spanish crown had the castle reconstructed. After 10 years of construction, the Castillo was completed in 1596. In 1991, after two years of renovation, the castle was converted into a museum.

Access is via a wide stone staircase with thick metal chains as railings, then via a small drawbridge and leads directly into the inner courtyard. On the left side, a little hidden, is the cash register. After payment you will receive a flyer with short information about the story.

The exhibition offers everything that could be collected here about pirates: Sailing ship models, including an 18th century warship with mini-cannons on board, an old ship's bell, a plumb bob, a sextant and, among other things, old revolvers.

Furthermore, colorful posters with short information about the following pirates decorate the rooms: Francis Drake, Jean Fleury, Woodes Rogers, Walter Reigeigh, Morato Arráez, Le Clerc and Sores, George Clifford, Robert Blake, Tabac Arraez and Soliman. The information on the posters is written in Spanish and English only.
In the basement of the building there will be a film screening entitled "Nelson en Canarias", as Admiral Nelson conquered Santa Cruz in Tenerife.
From the upper floor one has again a fantastic view over the whole island.

5.10 Monumento al Campesino - The farm monument
The **Monumento al Campesino is located** on the LZ-20 road in the municipality of San Bartolomé, in the geographical centre of the island, from where you have access to all points of the island. Already from a distance you can see the big white sculpture, which is the landmark of this place. It stands on a lava rock hill, is only 15 meters high, but immediately catches the eye.

After the design drawing by **César Manrique, which can** also be seen in the Fundación CM, the construction was realized in 1968 by Jésus Soto, his closest collaborator. The sculpture, welded together from water tanks of old fishing boats, is called a **fertility monument** and depicts a farmer with his herd of goats.

Directly behind the monument is the farming village. The complex is picturesquely white, small and well-kept. Follow the road to the right.

The rooms of the village are dedicated to the traditional crafts of the island.
Every day from 11.00 to 14.00 there will be workshops where the preparation of Canarian mojosauces and the preparation of gofio as a typical island dessert will be shown and explained.
For a contribution towards expenses of 3,00 € you can become active.
In the adjoining rooms there is also the possibility to take part in courses on authentic Canarian embroidery and pottery. Since the artists are often not present, only a view of the premises can be taken.

Price advantage: 2 courses cost 5,00 €, 3 courses 7,00 €.
On the upper floor you can see models of all the churches in Lanzarote, as well as clay figures, jugs and ensembles of figures by the artist Juan Brito Martín, who died in February 2018 at the age of 98.

In the souvenir shop one finds beside the normal souvenirs also different wines from 10 wineries of the island at reasonable prices: La Grieta, Martinon, El Grifo, Reymar, Vulcano, Rubicon, Vega del Yuco, Bermejos, Yaiza and Guiguan.
The large spiral staircase in the middle of the farming village leads through a "black hole" into the lower part of the complex. The subsequent lava entrance ends in a large restaurant, which is primarily used by organized bus tours for lunch break.

If one now climbs the big stairs, one gets to the café of the Monumento al Campesino.

The beautiful ambience invites you to linger. The prices are reasonable, so that on weekends you will mainly meet islanders. In addition to traditional dishes, the menu offers tapas typical of the island, a small selection of which is presented in the bar: marinated olives, pickled cheese and fish, marinated tuna cubes, stockfish, pulp, marinated tomatoes, Russian salad and tomatoes stuffed with tuna salad.

5.11 Casa Amarilla - Arrecife
Casa Amarilla, the yellow house, is located in Calle León y Castillo, at the beginning of the main shopping street in Arrecife.

The building was the former seat of the island government, which was built in the 1920s, declared a cultural asset of special interest in 2002 and renovated in 2014.
In the exhibition rooms temporally changing presentations take place, which reflect the history of the island.
Opening hours: Mon-Fri: 10:00- 22:00, Sat from 10:00- 14:00.
Further information on the current exhibition can be found at:
www.cactlanzarote.com

6   La Graciosa- The little pearl off Lanzarote
The 27 square kilometre small island lies on the north coast of Lanzarote. **La Graciosa** was uninhabited until the end of the 19th century, when a small fish factory was built and the first people settled there.

From that moment the inhabitants overcame the difficult living conditions that an island without drinking water, with strong winds and land difficult to cultivate brought with it. For years, traditional fishing was the only source of income that required crossing the **El Río**, the strait between Lanzarote and La Graciosa, to sell the fish and buy drinking water and other food from the proceeds.

Currently 700 people live on the island. In the summer months about 4000 tourists join us. The manageable village has 150 cars. In the capital **Caleta del Sebo you will** find a small medical centre, a post office, a pharmacy, a fish shop, the harbour administration, a health centre and 3 supermarkets. Recently, several restaurants have opened, as well as an Aloe Vera Museum.

La Graciosa can already be seen from Lanzarote. From Mirador del Río you can enjoy a fantastic view of the island and the uninhabited islands of Montaña Clara, Roque del Oeste and Alegranza.

From Órzola you can take the ferry from Lineas Maritimas Romero. There are sufficient parking facilities at the jetty, which are allocated by parking attendants. The crossing takes only 30 minutes.
The first 10 minutes are a bit wobbly, depending on the waves, after the big rocks at the end of Lanzarote the ship enters shallower waters.

Once in the port, you can explore the island on foot, by rental bike, or guided by jeep.
On foot it is only 700 m to the first beach El Salado, which can be covered in 10 minutes.
The second beach, La Francesa, which is located in the south, can be reached after 2.8 km in 40 minutes, and the southernmost beach, Playa de La Cocina, after 3.8 km in 55 minutes.
The southernmost peak El Pobre can be reached after 7.4 km in 2 hours.
To the El Corral depression, located in the west of the island, it is 4 km, which can be reached from the main town in 1 hour and 10 minutes.

To the beach Las Conchas it is 5.1 kilometres, for which one needs 1 hour and 20 minutes. To Pedro Barba it is 6.4 km, which one manages in 1.4 hours.
With the bicycle, the rental is directly opposite the jetty, it is of course faster, but one should consider that on the island it is only a matter of sandy paths. So it is 4 minutes to El Salado, 15 minutes to La Francesa, 30 minutes to El Corral, 35 minutes to Las Conchas, 40 minutes to Pedro Barba and 50 minutes to El Pobre. The jeep tours start on the right side of the harbour. There are one-way, return journeys to and from the beaches, which can be requested from the drivers depending on the distance and number of people.

Since the end of 2018 Graciosa now has the status of the 8 independent Canary Islands, after Lanzarote, Fuerteventura, Gran Canaria, Tenerife, La Palma, La Gomera and El Hierro.

6.1 La Graciosa- The complete island tour

The jeep departure station is located in the harbour on the right-hand side. Not as indicated on the poster, the authorized drivers make the whole island tour for 50,00 €. The tour for the right or left side of the island costs 50,00 € each, for the whole tour 100,00 € are required. The whole island tour includes the following places:
- Pedro Barba
- Playa Lambra
- Caleton de los Arcos
- Playa de las Conchas - half the island tour would go to here
- Baja Corral
- Caleton de las Hurtas
- Montaña Amarilla
- La Laguna
- Playa Francesa

The tour starts through the capital Caleta del Sebo of the island.

A sandy road leads through the village to Pedro **Baba**, a tiny village with small houses that are only inhabited during the summer months.

Pedro Barba was the first inhabited place on the island. At the end of the small settlement stands a house, which at that time housed a school for 4 pupils, behind it lies the cemetery.

After a short break we continue towards **Playa del Ambra.** This section of the island is comparable with the snow-white dune landscape in Corralejo, in the north of Fuerteventura, but as a miniature edition.

The next stop is in front of **Caleton de Los Arcos, where you will be guided on** foot by your guide. The natural spectacle is reminiscent of Los Hervideros on Lanzarote.

Continuing in the direction of **Montaña Bermeja,** along the coast, you will reach the beautiful sandy beach, **Playa de las Conchas.**

Via the **Baja del Corral** and the **Caleton de las Hutras the** tour leads to the **Montaña Amarilla**. As the track is not completely around the island, the jeep drives back the whole way, towards the starting point, with the new destination **Playa Francesa**.

Ferry times: www.lineasromero.com
Órzola- La Graciosa: 8.30/ 10.00/ 11.00/ 12.00/ 13.30/ 16.00/ 18.00. From 01 May to 31 October 19.00 and from 01 July to 20 October 20.00.
La Graciosa- Órzola: 8.00/ 8.40/ 10.00/ 11.00/ 12.30/ 15.00/ 16.00/ 17.00 hours, from 01 May to 31 October at 18.00 hours and from 01 July to 20 October at 19.00 hours.

7   Vineyard La Geria
La Geria, a wine-growing area of over 5 hectares, is located in the centre of the island, between Yaiza and San Bartolomé, on the edge of the Timanfaya National Park. It is the largest wine-growing area in the Canary Islands and has been declared a Nature Reserve.

During the severe volcanic eruptions between 1730 and 1736, a layer of volcanic ash up to 2 m thick was deposited in this area. This layer of small lava stones is called picón. It has the property that the small amount of moisture resulting from heavy cloud formation does not drain off, but seeps away immediately into the soil and can thus be absorbed by the plants.

The islanders benefited from this advantage, both then and now, for the cultivation of wine. In order to protect the vines from the continuous winds of varying intensity, a semi-circular low wall of lava stones was built around each plant. Thus the whole area of La Geria is covered by these stone semicircles surrounded in the middle by vines, up to the volcanic mountains.

The same procedure is still used today to cultivate cereals and vegetables, except that outside this area the lava stones are poured onto fields to make them usable. Therefore, one should not be surprised outside this area that one finds again and again large black lava fields.

The impressive drive through the wine-growing region takes you past many smaller and larger bodegas: El Campesino, El Grifo with wine museum, Stratus, Rubicon and La Geria.

Tip: Visit the **Bodega Los Bermejos with its** award-winning wines. At the Monumento al Campesino turn left towards La Geria onto the LZ-30. Shortly after the sign for El Islote, a fork in the road leads to the winery.

Wine tastings are offered on request. Los Bermejos is available in white, rosé and red, as well as sparkling wine. According to many Lanzaroteños it is the best wine of the island.

8 The Fire Mountains
8.1 Pilgrimage Church Ermita de Los Dolores

The sanctuary of **Ermita de Nuestra Señora de Los Dolores is considered to** be the centre of Marian worship in Lanzarote and is one of the most important in the Canary Islands. It is located in the town of Mancha Blanca, which belongs to the municipality of Tinajo.

According to history: In September 1730, the Timanfaya region opened up, and lava flows destroyed the villages and fertile valleys in the area. Volcanic eruptions started that lasted five years. In the year 1735 the glowing lava flows moved over the place Mancha Blanca towards Tinajo.

Fearing the destruction of their houses, the inhabitants of the village, in a procession led by the priest Esteban de la Guardia, approached the lava with the statue of the Virgen de Los Dolores.

One of the pilgrims rammed a heavy wooden cross into the ground in front of the lava flow and the lava came to a standstill. Out of gratitude, the inhabitants of Tinajo promised to build a pilgrimage church on this site for the Virgin.

Years later, the virgin appeared to the shepherdess Juana Rafaela and reminded her of this promise. In 1779 the inhabitants applied for permission to build the church, which was completed in 1782.

Every year the pilgrimage in honour of the Madonna takes place on 15 September. Since processing takes place on Saturdays, the date may be shifted by a few days.
In the church the priest holds Holy Mass, then the statue is carried in front of the church where the festivities begin.
On this day, the sleepy village is transformed into a mixture of procession, fair and market.

Many Lanzaroteños dress for the pilgrimage, the **Romería de Los Dolores, in** typical national costume and pilgrimage from their homes in groups on foot to Mancha Blanca.
In recent years, the colourful hustle and bustle has developed into an event with an attached small fair and several stalls. The **Feria de Artesania de Lanzarote, the** great artisan exhibition, also takes place at the same time.

TIP: The small, simple church is definitely worth a visit, as it belongs to the history of the island. If you are on the island around the 15th of September, ask for the exact date of the Romeria and watch the spectacle. Also interesting is the handicraft market, where not only the Lanzaroteños, but also the inhabitants of the neighbouring islands sell their works.
By the way: Since September 2016, the major tour operators have also been offering excursions to this artisan fair.

8.2 Timanfaya Visitor Centre- Centro de Visitantes

The **visitor centre is located** at the Timanfaya National Park. The large, white building complex immediately stands out from the dark lava and scree masses.

The beginning of the national park is easy to see, as the fire devil designed by César Manrique is enthroned on a lava stone mountain.
One encounters a large exhibition on volcanoes and a 30-minute film screening on volcanic eruptions.

Admission is free. The most spectacular thing about this center is that it is possible to simply sit on a bench in a lava field. At the end of the exhibition you go through the glass door, which is on the right-hand side, and reach a wooden walkway. This leads through an impressive dead still, almost unreal landscape. At the end of the footbridge there are two wooden benches that invite you to linger.

TIP: Sit down, enjoy the view up to the volcanoes and let your soul dangle... Absolutely recommendable is the **Tremesana hike, which** leads through the Timanfaya National Park and is offered free of charge by the centre.

8.3 Timanfaya Fire Mountains - Montañas del Fuego

The **Montañas del Fuego**, the Fire Mountains, or Timanfaya, are located in the southwest of the island and belong to a large area that was affected by volcanic eruptions between 1730 and 1736 and later in 1824. This long, eruptive process drastically changed the appearance of the island. Almost a quarter of Lanzarote was buried under a thick layer of lava and ash.

The volcanic landscape has a total area of 174 square kilometres, but the part protected as a national park, where the most significant eruptions took place, covers only 51 square kilometres. It stretches to the east, from the border of Yaiza to Montaña Timanfaya, the western border being the coast. 32 volcanic cones were formed here.

The special climatic conditions of the island led to the fact that the volcanic landscape is as good as still unchanged and the **Timanfaya area** was declared a **national park in 1974.**

Between the years 1726 and 1730 there were strong earthquakes and underground rumbling which caused panic among the inhabitants. In search of protection they went to Teguise and Arrecife. The eruption began towards the end of the summer of 1730, on the evening of the first of September. The events of that time have been recorded in the chronicles of an extraordinary witness, the **priest of Yaiza,** Don Andres Lorenzo Curbelo.

He described: "Between nine and ten o'clock in the evening the earth suddenly opened up near Timanfaya, only two miles from Yaiza. During the first night a huge mountain rose from the womb of the earth and from its summit escaped flames that "burned for 19 days".

This was the beginning of the most important volcanic process of the Canary Islands. It lasted for six years with varying intensities and was marked by lava flows, with a temperature of more than 800O and huge ash rain that wiped out all life.

In the parish priest's historical manuscript, the following report can be read: "On October 18, 1730, three new openings formed over Santa Catalina and from them came out steam masses that spread all over the island, accompanied by cinders and ashes that spread all over the surrounding area. The explosions that accompanied these phenomena, the darkness produced by ashes and the smoke that enveloped the entire island drove the inhabitants of Yaiza "to flight" more than once.

Today, almost 300 years later, more and more life pulsates in the middle of the lava. About 800 animal and plant species were registered. Most of it on land, the rest in the sea. Among the organisms that live directly on rocks are primarily birds, lizards and above all various lichen species, as well as some nocturnal insects that feed on microscopic particles carried by the wind. These are primarily beetles and crickets, which may have been very similar to the species that arrived on the island millions of years ago when Lanzarote emerged from the sea.

The last volcanic eruptions took place in 1824. They were preceded by a 10-year period during which numerous medium-intensity earthquakes were recorded on the island. The peculiarities of these eruptions were the thin liquid of the lava and the enormous columns of boiling saltwater, which were up to 30 meters above the surface of the craters and flooded the area.

In this phase, the last of the lava flows threatened the village of **Mancha Blanca**. Out of need, the inhabitants borrowed the statue of the Virgen de Los Dolores, the church in the neighbouring village of Tinajo. And the miracle happened. A wooden cross was rammed into the glowing lava, which came to a standstill shortly afterwards.

8.4 Isle of Hilario- Islote de Hilario

Along the Timanfaya, unusual temperatures originating from the earth developed on the surface, which volcanologists call geothermal anomalies. The centre is located at the top of the island of Hilario, where several performances are presented to the spectators.

Legend has it that the island is named after **Hilario from Lanzarote, who** lived there alone with his camel mare like a hermit. Hilario planted a fig tree that thrived but never bore fruit because "the flower could not feed on the flame".

A tribute to the legend can be found in the restaurant El Diablo. Inside you can see an open, glazed circle with camel bones and the branches of a fig tree on a black picon.

8.5 Timanfaya- Volcano route- La Ruta de los Volcanes

Inside the national park there is a 14 km long route which is **only** used by **bus.** It was realized in 1968 under the direction of César Manrique and his partner Jésus Soto. The road lines are harmoniously adapted to the landscape and run along the volcanic eruption zone. On the impressive tour you can see small ovens, caves and heavily eroded, dry infertile land.

Important information: After arriving in the National Park Timanfaya by car and paying the entrance fee, one drives up to the collecting parking place. There, one gets into the buses of the national park with the entrance ticket in order to be driven through the unique volcanic landscape. Contrary to some assertions, there is no other possibility. Guests who travel with organised bus journeys only get back on their coach, which departs on the same route.

By the way: Since 2016, tour operator TUI has been offering a special excursion in the evening hours, during which guests can get off the bus at a point in the National Park. This excursion is combined with a dinner at the Timanfaya restaurant, which is included in the price but does not allow any menu selection.

8.6 Timanfaya- Restaurant El Diablo
In 1970, under the direction of César Manrique, the **El Diablo restaurant was** built at the very point where the thermal anomalies were most severe.
It is located on the Islote del Hilario in the Timanfaya National Park and was built before the area was declared a National Park.

Cooking is done with natural geothermal energy. The kitchen stove is a six meter deep hole in the shape of a fountain that rises from the heat to cook the barbecue food on a large grill. Only materials that can withstand the high temperatures were used for the construction. The circular restaurant offers a fantastic view of the Timanfaya region through its large windows.

Specialities include half grilled chicken, sardines, marinated chicken legs, chicken breast, mixed skewers, entrecote, fillet of beef and lamb chops. Important: A visit to the restaurant is only possible in connection with the entrance fee for the national park.

8.7 Timanfaya National Park - on your own or organized?

Basically there are two ways to look at the mountains of fire: On your own in a rental car or with an organized bus trip.

The Timanfaya area is located in the southwest of Lanzarote and belongs to the municipality of Yaiza. The fire devil designed by César Manrique signals the beginning of the Timanfaya National Park, the Parque Nacional Timanfaya.

Depending on the rush of visitors, there can be long queues of cars after the ticket booth in the park, so that one has to be prepared for waiting times of up to almost one hour. With the coach it is easier, because they are let through immediately.

After the ticket counter, drive up to the parking lot, park the car and go towards the restaurant, before the demonstration by National Park employees take place.

In order to demonstrate the immense heat of the earth, small stones are placed in the hand. Afterwards gorse is burned and impressive water fountains are left from holes in the ground.

At the end of the demonstration, you will be taken to a giant barbecue where you will be able to grill chicken legs, skewers and sausages exclusively with geothermal energy in a six metre deep well.

Guests of the organized trips return to the coaches, the drivers change to the buses of the National Park. Unfortunately, it is no longer possible to drive through the area by car. The ticket is validated by the bus driver before departure.

Then follows a 45-minute journey through the fascinating Timanfaya landscape. The route travelled by organised coach or bus is the same.

In the Timanfaya bus a 3-language CD with the story of the volcanic eruptions with musical background is inserted now. The languages are Spanish, English and German.

After arriving at the terminus, you still have the opportunity to shop in the souvenir shop. In most cases, the guided tours leave their guests 30 minutes to drive on.

It is different for those who travel with their own vehicle. If you feel like it, you can watch the fire shows again, or eat in the restaurant "El Diablo".

Worth knowing: If you want to combine a visit to Timanfaya with a dinner, only organized bus excursions are possible, which can be booked locally. Note that these excursions may be multilingual and food is not offered à la carte.

8.8 Camel Ride - Echadero de los Camellos

The camel resting place, **Echadero de los Camellos**, is located on the main road that runs through the Timanfaya Nature Reserve.

Immediately one sees waiting camels, better said dromedaries and caravans, which set off with tourists on the humps, in order to get rocking through the lava landscape for a fee.

On the right side of the parking lot there is a small snack café with the possibility to buy souvenirs, public toilets, as well as a small free exhibition on the topic: Timanfaya and camels - how the animals were used to facilitate the work in agriculture.

9 Lago Verde- Laguna de los Clicos

In the south, just before the fishing village El Golfo, there is the **Lago Verde** with the **Laguna de los Clicos**. To discover the "green lake", drive down the road to El Golfo and park on the left just before entering the village.

The path begins at the end of the car park and leads uphill to the lake after about 10 minutes.

The lagoon is crescent-shaped in the arc of a partially submerged volcanic crater, about thirty metres from the coast. The lake owes its bright green colour to the influence of the Ruppia Maritima algae, which find optimal living conditions in the extremely salty waters of the lagoon.

Although the lagoon is subterraneously connected to the sea and is constantly replenished with fresh sea water, it evaporates more and more and has already lost a considerable part of its original size. The lake has been placed under nature protection and is cordoned off with ropes. Entering and bathing are not permitted. Nevertheless, one should not miss the colourful natural spectacle.
In the following fishing village El Golfo countless restaurants invite you to eat fish.

10   Los Hervideros
On the southwest coast, between the Janubio salt flats and the fishing village of El Golfo, there are the bizarre rock formations of **Los Hervideros**.

Hervidero means "bubbling", so it is obvious why this stretch of coast is called so. Especially when the rough high waves of the Atlantic hit the rock masses, it seems as if the water is still boiling.
The landscape was created during the last great volcanic eruptions between 1730 and 1736, when the hot lava masses of Timanfaya poured into the sea and solidified rapidly.
On narrow paths, one gets to the small, extended platforms from which one can observe the spectacle at close range.
Only when the surf is strong does one experience a fantastic natural spectacle of the approaching waves, which force themselves through the rock plates and shoot into the air as metre-high fountains. In the background the high volcanic craters of the Montañas del Fuego are impressive.

11   Saltworks of Janubio- Las Salinas de Janubio
On Lanzarote there are only two salt flats left, in the north the Salinas del Río, in the west the **Salinas de Janubio**. At the top of the main street you have a wonderful view over the whole complex.

The Janubio salt flats are the largest in the Canary Islands and one of the most important in the world. They have existed since 1895 and were designed by the salt maker Victor Fernandez. The complex was built of volcanic rock and is a listed building.

At that time the water was taken out of the lagoon by 5 windmills with paddle wheels standing on stone pedestals of different heights. In the meantime, this is done by electric motors.

The water runs through a main channel and reaches the various evaporation basins via secondary channels. This is followed by repeated transfer to other tanks, which increases the original salt content from 4 to 20 %. The water is then transferred to crystallization basins. After approx. 3 weeks the salt separates from the brine.

This process is repeated up to 14 times between March and October. The salt is dried and purified in lateral ditches until it comes to the next flooding of the basin. From November to February, the plant is being repaired.

Through the open entrance gate you drive down to the Salzbodega, the Bodega de la Sal.

From the slightly elevated platform you can view the saltworks from up close.

Tip: Profit from the manufacturer prices in the bodega with the largest offer of unusual, handmade sea salts.

are offered: **Sea salt** with volcanic activated carbon, flavoured herbs, chilli, lemon, guayonje onion from Tenerife, tomato, or red wine.
Seasoning salts for meat, fish, pasta and vegetables.

Sal Malvasía Volcánica with Malsavía wine and herbs
Sal condimentada al Mojo picón extra- extra hot with garlic, cumin, pepperoni and hot paprika
Sal condimentada al Cúrcuma with turmeric, garlic and oregano
Sal condimentada with thyme, garlic and oregano
Sal al Vino tinto with red wine and herbs
Sal al Mojo picón with spicy paprika, pepperoni and garlic
Sal condimentada al Curry mit Curry, Knoblauch und Oregano
Sal condimentada al Mojo verde with parsley, coriander, garlic and green pepper.

12   Lanzarote- Fuerteventura

Two islands so close together that they couldn't be more different. Already from Puerto del Carmen and many view points, one sees from the distance the snow-white dunes of Corralejo on **Fuerteventura**.

This is not surprising, as Fuerteventura is only 15 km away from Lanzarote. There are several possibilities to see the snow white sand, the huge sand dunes and the turquoise water:
The easiest is to book an organized excursion with the destination Fuerteventura - Corralejo and the dunes. With the glass bottom boat it goes from the harbour in Playa Blanca to Fuerteventura. Mostly, a shopping stop is made in the centre of Corralejo, after which one is driven with the group in the bus to the dunes and to the beach. After further availability with the possibility of bathing, one is brought back to the port of Corralejo, transfers again by boat and is brought to the hotels on Lanzarote.

The second possibility would be to translate to Fuerteventura by car ferry from Armas or Fred Olsen in only 30 minutes, or by glass bottom boat in about 45 minutes. Arrived at Fuerteventura, one takes a taxi from the harbour or takes the public bus to the dunes. The taxi prices are humane as the dunes are not too far away. The bus station is located directly at the back of the harbour building.

If one has already rented a car on Lanzarote, there is the option to take the car to Fuerteventura for one day, depending on the rental car company. This would be the easiest and most independent way to explore the island, but the price for the crossing plus car should be considered and compared with the ferry operators.

Ferry times and prices at www.navieraarmas.com or www.fredolsen.es

Armas: Playa Blanca- Corralejo: 7.00- 9.00- 11.00- 13.15- 15.00- 17.00- 19.00 hours

Corralejo- Playa Blanca: 8.00- 10.00- 12.00- 14.00- 16.00- 18.00- 20.00 hours

Daily, but on Sundays and public holidays Armas does not offer the routes Playa Blanca - Corralejo at 13.15 and 15.00, and back from Corralejo- Playa Blanca, at 12.00 and 14.00.

Fred Olsen:

Playa Blanca- Corralejo: from Monday to Friday: 7.10- 8.30- 10.00- 12.30- 14.00- 16.00- 18.00 and Saturday and Sunday: 8.30- 10.00- 14.00- 16.00- 18.00.

Corralejo- Playa Blanca: from Monday to Friday: 7.45- 9.00- 11.00- 13.30- 15.00- 17.00- 19.00 and Saturday and Sunday: 9.00- 11.00- 15.00- 17.00- 19.00.

Important: For the crossing you need an identity card or passport!

Conclusion: If you have never been to Fuerteventura before, you should definitely have a look at the Canarian favorite island of the German beach vacationers. The huge snow-white dune landscape around Corralejo and the turquoise water alone are a feast for the eyes. To get to the beaches, follow the signs for Playas Grandes. Here you will find the most beautiful beaches of the north, located at the level of the two large RIU hotels.

Unfortunately, it is not possible to sufficiently explore Fuerteventura with the rental car in one day, as the island is too long. From the northernmost point in Corralejo, you drive to the southernmost point in Morro Jable, over 2 hours, which is only possible without any stop. Therefore I recommend to stay in the north of Fuerteventura and enjoy a nice day at the beach. Don't forget your bathing suit!

13   César Manrique- a unique artist

Today's Lanzarote would be unthinkable without the enormous influence of **César Manrique.** He was not only a painter, architect and sculptor, but also an active environmentalist and had a decisive influence on the image of the volcanic island. It is thanks to him that the beauty of Lanzarote did not sink into mass tourism, but was emphasized by a harmonious combination of art and nature.

César Manrique was born on 24 April 1919 in Arrecife. He grew up with his twin sister, his brother and another sister in Puerto Naos, the old port of Arrecife.

A carefree childhood and the summer holidays with his family in Caleta de Famara, a small fishing village in the northwest, had a lasting influence on him.
During the Spanish Civil War, from July 1936 to April 1939, Manrique volunteered to fight alongside Franco, later dictator General Francisco Franco. After the war he returned to Arrecife, immediately banished his uniform and never spoke again about the cruel time of war and the memories connected with it.

Already in 1942, at the age of 23, he presented works in his first exhibition in the capital of the island.

He enrolled in Tenerife, the oldest university in the Canary Islands, in the field of technical architecture and dropped out after 2 years.

In 1950, after five years of study, he completed his second degree at the Academy of Fine Arts in Madrid with the title of Master of Drawing and Painting.
He married Pepi Gomez with whom he had a close relationship until her death in 1963.
With like-minded artists, Manrique developed into a pioneer of avant-garde art and opened Spain's first gallery for abstract art in Madrid in 1954.

In 1964, at the age of 45, he received a scholarship from the International Institute of Art Education in America.

In New York three exclusive solo exhibitions took place in the gallery "Catherine Viviano".
For his further development as an artist, representatives of abstract expressionism, Pop Art (Andy Warhol), the new sculpture and kinetic art were decisive. After 4 years in the USA, he became homesick in 1966 and decided to return to Lanzarote to transform his home island into one of the most beautiful places in the world.

Already in Tenerife and Gran Canaria a merciless building boom had taken place in the form of huge hotel castles and interventions in the landscape, which now threatened to destroy Lanzarote. Manrique was able to win over a long-time friend of the family, Pepin Ramirez, who was now president of the island government, for his project. Only the traditional, maximum two-storey construction method should be permitted and a ban on advertising posters on the island should be introduced. This ban has been enforced, but has since been lifted.

In order to pass on the Lanzarote architectural style to his compatriots, Manrique took the initiative and drove his car across the island to convince everyone of the original architecture.

In the same year, he designed the Monumento al Campesino, the 15-metre-high monument, welded together from the water tanks of old fishing boats, dedicated to working farmers. His closest partner Jésus Soto realized the monument.
Together with his artist friend Luis Ibánez, he bought an old house in Yaiza, one of three that had stood still after the volcanic eruptions from 1730 to 1736, and converted it into the restaurant La Era in 1970.

In the same year he discovered a fig tree in a black lava field in Tahiche, the green tip of which protruded from a lava flow. He decided to build his house right here. The landowners did not demand payment for their land because they considered it worthless and asked Manrique to take as much land as he needed for his project. During the construction phase, Manrique discovered five underground lava bubbles, which he connected, expanded and transformed into living spaces.

In 1974, Manrique opened the EL Almacen multi-purpose cultural centre in Arrecife, which was to serve as a meeting place for art lovers. Artists should have the opportunity to exhibit their works in the El Aljibe Art Gallery.
In 1982 he founded his foundation, the Fundacíon César Manrique.
In 1988 he moved out of the house in Tahiche to move into his converted farmhouse in Haría, which has been a museum since 2013.

On 25 September 1992, César Manrique died in a traffic accident just 50 metres from his foundation in Tahiche. At the intersection where he had crossed a stop sign, there is now a roundabout with a wind chime designed by him. He was buried in the cemetery of Haría. His twin sister died on 13.11.2018.

The following buildings, designed by César Manrique, can be visited:
The **Casa Museo del Campesino**, a farmhouse complex with typical island architecture, with the **Monumento al Campesino**, a monument located on the geographical centre of the island to honour the farmers of Lanzarote who discovered that the black lava stones are porous and can thus absorb the dew to irrigate the fields.

The **Lagomar**, the residential complex of Omar Sharif and the viewpoint **Mirador del Río with** view to the neighbouring island La Graciosa.

The **Jameos del Agua**, a lagoon inside a lava cave that houses a blind albino crayfish, as well as a concert hall with 600 seats and the cactus garden, the **Jardín de Cactus**, with more than 1000 cactus species.

The **Fundación César Manrique**, his house with 5 underground lava bubbles and his last residence the **Casa/ Museo César Manrique.**

The **restaurant El Diabolo** in the Timanfaya National Park, amidst the active fire mountains, with a large grill about volcanic air and the **Castillo San José** with the **Museo Internacional de Arte Contemporaneo**, a contemporary museum with a changing art exhibition and the integrated restaurant **Que Muac**.

The **Hotel Meliá Las Salinas** in Costa Teguise, designed for the César Manrique garden, walls and pool area, as well as the **Jugetes del Viento,** wind chimes, which are located in his Fundación and on many roundabouts of the island.

14   The Great César Manrique Tour
Discover the fantastic versions of a man who made Lanzarote what it is today, unique and unmistakable.
Follow in the footsteps of César Manrique:
- Mirador del Río
- Cuevas de los Verdes
- Jameos del Agua
- Jardín de Cactus
- Hotel Melía Salinas in Costa Teguise
- Fundacíon César Manrique
- Lagomar
- Casa Museo- Monumento al Campesino
- Castillo San José
- Casa/ Museo César Manrique
- Timanfaya National Park

15   Beaches- Las Playas
Lanzarote is not the beach paradise with infinitely long, bright beaches. Due to the tides of the Atlantic Ocean, all beaches can be used, but in many cases bathing is only possible at high tide.

At low tide the sea goes back so far that sometimes only black stones or black lava flows that go into the sea remain. Thus the so-called "beach life" has in most cases two faces. On the one hand, a wow effect develops at high tide, so that one is pleased about the crystal clear sea and turquoise play of colours. On the other hand, at low tide, when the black, thick stones appear in the sea, one thinks that a truck has arrived that has unloaded boulders.

So many holidaymakers who are on Lanzarote for the first time say that they have never imagined it that way and that everything is terrible. Nevertheless, both high and low tide have their own special visual appeal.

On Lanzarote most beaches are of fine sand, a few of coarse or a mixture of sand and stones. Mostly, one finds light sand, but there are also brown and black sand beaches.

In the holiday regions Costa Teguise, Puerto del Carmen, Playa Blanca and in the capital, sunbeds and parasols are offered for a fee. There is enough space between the lounger areas to sit down with your own beach towel. This is the only place you should go swimming, as lifeguards are on duty. **Please never underestimate the extremely strong undercurrents of the Atlantic, which cost countless lives every year.**

Water temperatures are around 24o from July to September and can drop to 17o in the winter months.
The outside temperatures are highest in summer and are up to 35o in the shade during the day and 25o in the evening. A fleece jacket is recommended in the evening hours, bearable by a mild or strong wind, depending on the weather conditions.
In the summer months the UV value is 12, in the winter months 4-5. Do not underestimate this radiation and protect yourself with a sun cream with sufficient sun protection factor. Caution is advised, as the wind usually causes you to notice much too late how aggressive the sun is.
In the north, after the Jameos del Agua, towards Órzola, there are eight different bathing bays. As these beaches are located outside the tourist centres, the journey must be made by car.
The entire north coast in this zone belongs to the Malpais de la Corona, which is characterized by a low rocky coast with small bays and snow-white sand and contrasts

fantastically with the black volcanic landscape. A feast for the eyes that seeks its equal.
The bright bays have carved themselves into the black landscape and continue into the interior in the form of white dunes.

Playa del Caleton Blanco is the largest of these bays. The snow-white sandy beach is about five hundred metres long and, coming from Orzola, is located shortly after the small red road sign with the inscription LZ-1 KM 32, on the left side. The car can be parked directly in front of the beach. There are no sunloungers, but there are semicircular walls made of stacked lava stones in which you can lie sheltered from the wind.

Tip: If you want to spend the day here, it is best to take a sunshade, towels, sunscreen and drinks with you.

Unfortunately, in the summer months the beautiful bay with a view of Orzola and Monte Corona is very crowded. The Lanzaroteños spend a whole weekend here with child and cone, camping and grilling. Please note that you can only swim here at high tide, as the sea is only knee-deep at low tide.

The lonely **Playa del Risco** lies below the Salinas del Río.

If you are just before the Mirador del Río, turn left into the narrow road. On the right side you have a wonderful view to the island La Graciosa that lies before Lanzarote. The road is quite straight and moves curvy downwards. Shortly after an old wall, the first one on the right side, a right-left curve follows, on the left side one looks at a hotel finca. Exactly after this bend, just before the finca, you turn right after an accumulation of lava covered with lichens, before the power poles start.

If you see a jerky path with black paved lava stones, you are in the right place. Now you drive the way to the end and park the car. Then unfortunately the most difficult part follows. The beach, which is about one kilometre long and lonely, is extremely difficult to access.

At least you should wear sneakers, even better would be hiking shoes, otherwise you can only get to the upper platform, which is about 15 minutes away.

The path then descends steeply and scree-like without railings. According to two sporty young men, the descent to the beach takes one hour. The way back is correspondingly more difficult and takes one and three-quarter hours. One should have looked at Playa del Risco at least from the platform that is still relatively easy to reach. By the way, the men found it "so amazing", but said that you have to do something like this only once in your life, so that a repetition was excluded.

Playa de Famara is a beach almost three kilometres long with light brown sand, located at the foot of the Famara cliffs. Due to high waves and strong winds it is mainly used by kite- and windsurfers.

Playa La Santa Sport is a nearly one kilometre long, artificially created, bright sandy beach near the sports facilities of Club La Santa.

The beaches or rocky coast with bathing plateaus **Charco del Palo** and **Los Cocoteros, located at the** level of the cactus garden, are nudist zones.

On the **Costa Teguise there are** five bays of different sizes, all located on the beach promenade.

Playa Ancla, a small bathing bay, is located in front of the large Occidental Hotel Lanzarote Beach, at the entrance to the village.

Playa Bastian is located at the beginning of the Costa Teguise, directly at the promenade. The path is well signposted. The 400 m long beach with dark sand is mostly used by locals.

The **Playa de Jabillo** is a small bathing bay with a bright sandy beach that is crossed by rocks and that is located at the promenade in front of the Occidental Grand Hotel Teguise.

Playa de las Cucharas is the largest beach on the Costa Teguise. The approximately 600 meters long bright sandy beach is divided by a long breakwater that runs perpendicular to the bay. This means that swimming in the sea is also possible at low tide. The section to the left of the breakwater, in front of Hotel Melía Salinas, turns into a sea of black stones at low tide.

Playa de los Charcos is located directly in front of Hotel Lanzarote Beach and has a bright sandy beach. Due to cooled lava flows it is only possible to swim in the sea at high tide.

In the area of **Arrecife, there are** two beaches. **Playa del Reducto** is the 500 m long city beach of Arrecife, which is located right next to the Grand Hotel Arrecife at the promenade. The beautiful bright sandy beach, with turquoise water, invites you to take a long bath at high tide.

Playa de Guacimeta is an almost two kilometre long beach with fine, light brown sand in **Playa Honda**, located between Arrecife and the airport. It is primarily used by islanders and residents.
In the area of **Puerto del Carmen there are** 3 big sandy beaches:
Playa de Matagorda lies in front of the settlement of Matagorda and is a light brown sandy beach interspersed with stones.

Playa de Los Pocillos is located just before Puerto del Carmen on the beach promenade and is a more than one kilometre long, very deep brown sandy beach. **Playa Grande** is the main beach of Puerto del Carmen with light brown sand, which passes directly under the beach promenade in Puerto del Carmen.

At the end of Puerto del Carmen lies the small bay **Playa Chica.**

The **Playa de Quemada** is a dark stone beach that is located in the place **Playa Quemada**. From here, one can reach Playa Blanca in five to six hours via a hiking path, passing two further bays.

In the south of the island are the **Papagayo beaches, which are** composed of the bays **Playa Mujeres**, **Playa del Pozo**, **Playa de la Cera**, **Puerto Muela** and **Caleta del Congrio.** The one hundred to four hundred metre long sandy beaches are separated from each other by high cliffs. You can reach it by following the signs to Papagayo in Playa Blanca. A long jerky gravel road leads to a cash box with a barrier. The entrance fee per vehicle is € 3,00. After payment the piste leads to the beaches.

In **Playa Blanca you can** find 3 more bathing bays, **Playa Dorada**, the one in front of the hotel Princesa Yaiza, **Playa Flamingo**, a bay protected by square concrete blocks, which is situated in front of the big Iberostar complex Lanzarote Park. The **city beach is located** in the center of Playa Blanca.

In the southwest of the island, between the Salinas de Janubio and El Golfo, there are other beaches where you can swim at your own risk. **Playa de Janubio** is a long, dark sandy beach that separates the saltworks from the sea. After Los Hervideros follows the Charco de los Clicos with a small lake and a black stone beach at the end of El Golfo.

16   Shopping - Shopping
Lanzarote is not a shopping paradise that would make the heart of die-hard shopping lovers beat faster.
In the big holiday resorts Costa Teguise, Puerto del Carmen and Playa Blanca there are mainly souvenir shops, in the small shopping centres, the **Centros Comerciales**, Chinese and Indians offer plagiarisms of current brands.
On beaches and promenades the same is done by African sellers.
Branded goods, which are exclusively offered in specialist shops, can be purchased either in the capital Arrecife or in the big shopping centres.
The largest shopping centre on the island, **DEILAND, is located** between Arrecife and the airport on the LZ-2 motorway.

All current shops can be found at: www.deilandplaza.com/tiendas/

The **BIOSFERA PLAZA** in Puerto del Carmen, is the second largest shopping center.

All current shops can be found at: www.biosferaplaza.es
In the harbour of **Puerto Calero there is** a small, manageable shopping street with more exclusive brand shops.

You can find the current business at: www.caleromarinas.com
In the south of the island, the **MARINA RUBICON** shopping centre was renovated and reopened.

On the ground floor there are some specialist shops, but in the marina you can shop more extensively. All current shops can be found at: www.ccmarinalanzarote.com/tiendas/
On October 1, 2015, **H&M** opened its first store on Lanzarote in the Deiland shopping center. The well-known sports shop Decathlon **was** added with a large hall in Arrecife, at LZ-3 exit 4, in October 2016.

Important for shopping in the capital **Arrecife** are the opening hours, which differ from those of the shopping centres: The shops are usually open from Monday to Friday from 10.00 to 14.00, after lunch from 17.00 to 20.00 and on Saturdays from 10.00 to 14.00. Sundays are closed. On the other hand, the shopping centres are open daily from 10.00 to 22.00 hours.

Note: Just like in Germany, the stores have spring, summer, autumn and winter collections. For summer clothing one finds genuine bargains starting from in the middle of August, the winter sales starts on 06 January and ends at the beginning of of of March. Oversizes for ladies are available, besides H&M, from the Spanish companies Encuentro up to size 46 and Punta Roma up to size 54.

TIP: Chic Spanish fashion at affordable prices can be found in the Deiland shopping centre at the **Cortefiel** chain, which also offers a more exclusive collection under **Pedro del Hierro. You can take** a look at the collection on the website: www.cortefiel.com

16.1 Tobacco products- Cigarettes
Tobacco products are available in supermarkets and tobacco shops. Even if the prices in the airplane seem favorable, they are cheaper locally. Due to the low taxation, the price per bar starts at approx. 17,00 €. Individually sold cigarette packs, or from the vending machine are somewhat more expensive, since there is no price marking.

Important: On the return journey to Germany only 1 pole per person from 18 years, may be introduced. In order to pass through customs without any problems, please make sure that there is only 1 bar in the suitcase, as the luggage is considered personal.

16.2 Perfumeries- Profumerías
Perfume and cosmetics are also much cheaper in the Canary Islands than in Germany. In order not to fall for plagiarism, you should shop in perfumeries and compare prices beforehand.

16.3 Pharmacy- Farmacia
Almost all **medicines** are cheaper than in Germany. Even without a prescription you can easily get the medicine with a opened box.

16.4 Food
In the holiday areas you will find small supermarkets of the Spar and Dino chains at almost every corner, offering everything you need in addition to the hotel offer. Larger purchases at lower prices are better made in the large branches of the Spanish chains EuroSpar, Hiperdino or Mercadona.

The German supermarket chain LIDL is represented on Lanzarote with 3 branches in Arrecife, Playa Honda and Puerto del Carmen.

16.5 Vvalue added tax
The prices indicated in the shops are final prices. It should be noted that for food and drinks in bars and restaurants, if not specified, an additional 7% VAT is added to the indicated price. Hotels and Manrique Tourist Centres show only the final price on menus and drinks.

16.6 Marina Lanzarote
Opened in 2014, **Marina Lanzarote is located** in Avenida Olof Palme, near the Charco de San Ginés, on the outskirts of the capital, Arrecife.

The modern marina is a combination of **restaurants** and **shops that** pass directly by the marina. The complex can be reached on foot via a bridge, direct parking is directly behind.

The marina is not really accepted despite the busy public traffic by cruise ships, so that many shops and restaurants are now empty. Almost alone, the **Burger King** with his drive-in, which is called AUTOKING, meets with lively interest. For **night owls we** recommend the discotheque **Kopas**, where party goers meet on Fridays and Saturdays from 00.00 o'clock.

17   Overview Markets- Mecados- Mercadillos
Every day of the week there are markets on the island.
Mondays to Fridays:
From 09.00 to 14.00 there is a market in Arrecife in La Recova in the inner courtyard of the town hall. Access to the island's oldest market square is from Manuel Miranda Street and de la Liebre Street. Above the entrance there is a sign with the inscription La Recova.
Tuesdays:
09.30- 14.00: Farmer's market in Pueblo Marinero in Costa Teguise. The market consists of several small stalls selling fruit, vegetables, olives, goat cheese, wine and bananas.
10.00 - 14.00: Weekly market at the marina of Puerto Calero
Wednesdays:
10.00 - 14.00: Market at the Marina Rubicon in Playa Blanca
18.00- 22.30: Handicraft market at Pueblo Marinero in Costa Teguise
Thursdays:
09.00 - 14.00: Farmer's market on the square in front of the cultural centre Santiago del Mayor in Taíche.

Fridays:
10.00 - 14.00: Handicraft market in the pedestrian area of Arrecife around Calle Léon y Castillo
10.00 - 14.00: Weekly market at the marina of Puerto Calero
16.00 - 22.00: Large market in the old port of Varadero, Plaza de la Tiñosa, in Puerto del Carmen
18.00- 22.00: Handicraft market at Pueblo Marinero in Costa Teguise

Saturdays:
09.00 - 14.00: Small grocery market in Uga next to the church
09.00- 14.00 h: Recova market in Arrecife
09.00 - 13.00: Saturday market in the city centre of Arrecife around the church San Ginés
10.00 - 14.00: Market at the Marina Rubicon in Playa Blanca
10.00 - 14.00: handicraft market in front of the church in the centre of Haría

Sundays:
09.00 - 14.00: Small grocery market in Uga next to the church
10.00 - 14.00: Giant market with over 500 stalls in Teguise
10.00 - 13.00 h: Farmer's market in Mancha Blanca

17.1 Teguise Market - Mercadillo Teguise

The **Mercadillo Teguise takes place** every Sunday from 10.00 - 14.00 in **Teguise**, the former capital of the island. The village is sleepy on weekdays and on Sundays it is transformed into a huge market with over 500 stalls. It is the **highlight** on the island, from 11.00 a.m. the crowds push along the stands, as the selection is huge.

On the square in front of the church a **folklore group performs** dances in typical national costumes to self-played music around 11.30 a.m.. The church is open and can be visited.

Arrival and departure to the market: Arrival can be by rental car, public transport, taxi or organised trips.

Guarded, paid parking spaces are available on the main road for motorists. Arriving by public transport or by taxi is not a problem, but the return journey could be longer due to the mass volume.

Organized bus trips to the market are advantageous as they offer a guaranteed seat in the bus.

Tip for motorists: At the Campo de Fútbol, which is already recognizable from a distance by its high metal posts, there are free parking spaces.

17.2 Arts and crafts market in Haría

Every **Saturday, the** Mercado **de Artesanía takes** place from 10.00 to 14.30 on the village square in front of the church.

The market was created in 2001 to promote the sale of artisanal, regional and organic products and to offer visitors a wide choice.

At the now up to 70 different stalls, you can stroll past and shop in peace.

With so many products, it shouldn't be difficult to find the right souvenir.

TIP: Combine a Saturday excursion to the market with a visit to the **Museo de Arte Sacro** next to the church. Following this street, you will meet the artist of the **Autenica Ceramica Canaria on the** main road, who still burns his clay works in the village oven himself.

The Casa/ Mueso César Manrique, the last residence of the island artist, is signposted and within walking distance. On the same road, shortly after the property, you can buy the **last basket weaver of the island** unique basket weaving work.

By the way: In the cemetery of Haría, the Cementerio, which is also signposted, one finds the last resting place of César Manrique.

18   Gastronomy

The climate and the geographical position of the island have determined the development of the little varied agriculture, whose products, combined with those from the sea, were the basis of the traditional island cuisine.

Due to the tourism boom of the last decades, the variety of dishes has increased without losing the traditional cuisine.
The typical island fish, gilthead, sama and vieja are prepared in a wide variety of flavours. There is also goat and rabbit meat, served with cooked "papas arrugadas", the Canary shriveled potatoes, with red and green mojo sauce.

Typical island dishes include stews, potajes, stockfish, sancocho and ropa vieja, a stew of meat, potatoes, vegetables and chickpeas.
Also the goat cheese must be mentioned, which is produced after old tradition in many variants. Finally, no good wine from the wine-growing areas between Mozaga and La Geria should be missing.
Gofio, a roasted maize flour, barley, millet and wheat have always been the staple foods of Canarians. Gofio is now used to bind stews and to make desserts.

18.1 Products
Despite a lack of water, heat and winds laden with Saharan sand, Lanzarote produces a relatively large variety of products. Currently, fruit and vegetables such as onions, tomatoes, potatoes, sweet potatoes, watermelons and pumpkins are cultivated on an area of approx. 7,000 hectares.
Together with Fuerteventura, the island was for a long time known as the Canary Islands' granary, as grain and maize were cultivated in the sandy fields in the centre of the island.

Livestock breeding is limited primarily to goats, sheep and cows. The goat stands out here because it is additionally bred for milk production in order to produce goat cheese. The cheese is rich in proteins, calcium, phosphorus and vitamins A, B and D. About five litres of milk are needed to produce one kilo.

18.2 Fishing

In the past, the island's fishing fleet was the most important of the Canary Islands, with Arrecife, La Graciosa, Puerto del Carmen and Playa Blanca. Fishing rods and nets were used to catch fish such as tuna, pike, mackerel, grouper, hake and wreckfish.

Until the 20th century, the most common way of processing fish on the island was to salt it, so that Lanzarote could benefit from this method of processing due to its countless salt works at that time.

18.3 Traditional dishes

Canarian cuisine is Mediterranean. The most important meal is lunch. There are many possibilities and especially on Lanzarote there are still traditional dishes offered, as they have always been eaten on the island. It's not long before one notices the important relation to the sea: fish soup, stockfish, fish with onions... The stockfish, the Sancocho, is one of the most important dishes of the Canary Islands and is served in most cases with moy sauces and gofio.

The meat dishes come from the Canary Islands cattle breeding. One meets goat meat and rabbit in different sauces. Broths and stews are also classic traditional dishes.

Unfortunately, there is no typical liqueur as it is known from the other islands. The Lanzaroteños brew their liqueurs at home, or fall back on well-known brands of the neighboring islands.

19 Tapas- the little delicacies

Originally, the term **tapas** was derived from the Spanish word tapar, which means to cover. In bars, small snacks were placed on the beer or wine glasses to protect the drinks from flies.

If one speaks of tapas in the meantime, this refers exclusively to the portion size. As tapas all dishes can be served, be it olives, cheese, meatballs, potatoes, chickpeas, fish or meat. In Spanish, the names of the tapas sound much more sonorous when one speaks of Aceitunas, Queso, Albondigas, Papas arrugadas, Garbanzas, Pescado or Carne.

Therefore, in local restaurants, if a map is available, you will find a reference to tapas, a small portion, a ½ racion, half a portion, or a whole portion, a racion.

19.1 Restaurant recommendation Casa Félix- La Aulaga
The **restaurant Casa Felix is located** at the beach Playa Bastian, in the Calle Rosa, 4 in Costa Teguise, above the parking lot, to which 2 further restaurants connect.
The rustically furnished restaurant was opened on 27 August 1987 and has a terrace with tables from which you can marvelously see the sea.

The tapas offered include: Canarian style potatoes, fried sweet potatoes, small peppers, fried anchovies, fried fish or chicken chopsticks, fish or chicken croquettes, chickpea stew with meat, fish salad, fried sardine fillets, marinated tuna, fried moraine, fried squid with green sauce, fried cheese with fig jam, dwarf squid, tortilla española, goulash, chicken legs, pork, minced meat balls, Russian salad and dates with breakfast bacon.
TIP: Order a selection... everything is served on a large plate with Canarian sauces.

19.2 Restaurant recommendation Restaurante Monumento al Campesino
The restaurant is located in a farming village designed by **César Manrique, which also** owns the striking **Monumento al Campesino**, located on LZ-20 in San Bartolomé.

Passing the farm monument, which represents a farmer with a herd of goats, you go straight ahead, down the stairs and immediately meet the restaurant. It is possible to take a seat outside or inside.

19.3 Restaurant recommendation Bar Stop
The restaurant **Bar Stop** with **local cuisine is located at the** main street in Yaiza and is almost directly opposite the church at the Plaza **Nuestra Señora de los Remedios**.

It is possible to sit at five tables in the small restaurant. A menu does not exist, but there is a counter where you can choose the food.

Conclusion: The **top address for** anyone who wants to try **real local food**. An authentic ambience, with no frills or frills regarding the presentation. Friendly, quick staff who speak some English. Measured by the portion size, the prices are unbeatable. Even without knowledge of the language, you can choose the food in the display case by pointing to the food and simply saying tapa - small portion, or ración- large portion. **By the way:** the food changes daily and if the "pots" are empty, one has had bad luck.

Tip: Visit the restaurant punctually at 13.00 o'clock, because it is always very well visited, so that you rarely get a seat later.

19.4 Restaurant recommendation El Diablo- Timanfaya

The restaurant designed by César Manrique is located in the **Timanfaya National Park**.

TIP: Round off the Timanfaya excursion in the national park with a special meal, as fish and meat are cooked here over the large volcano oven. In an incomparable atmosphere, with a view of the volcanoes, just enjoy it! Please note the opening hours of the restaurant, which are displayed on Tripadvisor.

20   Gastronomy Events

The largest variety of tapas can be found at the two largest tapas events on the island.

20.1 Canary Island Day - The capital celebrates its independence

The Canary **Islands Day is** celebrated annually on 30 May, the year in which the Canary Islands gained autonomy in 1982. On this day the shops in the city centre of Arrecifes are closed. According to the motto Arrecife vive Canarias, Arrecife lives and celebrates the Canary Islands, in the park Parque José Ramirez Cerdá, right next to the big tourist information pavilion, a big party from 12.00 - 24.00 o'clock takes place.

The special: Countless stands of different restaurants are set up where you can get tapas and drinks for **1,00 €** each. In the Canarian colours yellow, red and white flutter ribbons are stretched over the whole square. In the middle there is a stage where groups make music in traditional costumes.

From 12.30 p.m. the whole square fills up and there is a folk festival atmosphere. Everything smells deliciously like food and you don't even know where to go first. **Feeling 1000 different tapas** waiting to be tried.
If not here, then where? More than you could imagine: Bocadillos rolls, pizza, skewers, cheese, sweets, paella, empanada dumplings, caracoles snails, gabanzana chickpea stew, gazpacho cold vegetable soup, papas potatoes, escalopines schnitzel... and a lot of things you haven't seen in restaurants before.

Tip: It is best to visit the festival immediately from 12.00 noon and get an overview of what you would like to try and get hold of, as crowds of people are already forming in front of the stands around 14.00 noon. Otherwise, just throw yourself into the crowd and enjoy the turbulent hustle and bustle until midnight like the locals and celebrate with them.

Note: The festival takes place every year on a Saturday. If the 30th of May does not fall on a Saturday, the event will be postponed before or after, depending on the permission of the municipality. It is best to ask at a tourist information office or at the hotel reception desk for the exact date of the event.

20.2 Festival Enogastronómico in Teguise
Every year at the end of November, the huge gastronomic festival takes place in Teguise that can also be described as a **tapas tasting mile**.

At well **over 100 stands,** restaurants, cheese dairies, wineries, bakeries and pastry shops, ice-cream parlours and other shops, tapas and wines are offered for tasting. Mainly visited by Lanzaroteños, there is a hustle and bustle and one literally pushes oneself past the stands to see which tapas are offered.

In order to taste tapas or wine, you must buy tickets at stands marked **Venta de Bebidas y Tickets**, Drinks and Tickets. The choice seems to be limitless.

The tapas offer is also interesting, presented by the **neighbouring islands El Hierro, Tenerife, Fuerteventura** and **La Palma.**
Tip: If you are on the island at the end of September, check the tourist information offices or the hotel for the exact date of the event. On Sundays you can combine the Tapas Festival in Teguise with a visit to the market.

21 museums
21.1 Museum Tanit- Museo Tanit
The ethnological **museum Tanit is** signposted in the centre of San Bartolomé.

It is family owned and located in former wine cellars of a traditional Canarian house dating from 1735.
The founders of the museum, Mr. José Ferrer Perdomo and Mrs. Remy de Quintana Reyes, have collected all kinds of objects and information for countless years in order to preserve Lanzarote customs and traditions, starting from their ancestors, the majos, until today for posterity.
In the entrance area a binder with all information about the museum will be handed out.

Family heirlooms from the last century have been collected and now almost daily objects have been collected which are sorted and exhibited according to themes.

These include, among other things: A music corner, millstones, stone mortars, volcanic stone basins, bars, an art gallery, a wine cellar used since 1780, camel baskets, threshing boards, a typewriter, wine press, paintings, a Canarian still, Bookcases with brochures from 1912, the patron saint of the island, the Virgen de los Dolores, ceramics, ethnography, a stone cheese mould, rush fabric, a bridal couple from Mojon in traditional clothes, a water depot, a threshing floor, a Canarian wine cellar and the garden. In the courtyard there is a small chapel dedicated to Nuestra Señora de Pino.

The **museum** is **self-financed** and is not supported by the island government. The proceeds from the entrance fees are used for the extension and preservation of the object, so that it is admirable that the founder visits the museum almost every day to expand the collection. **Opening hours:** Daily from 10.00 - 14.00, children up to 12 years are free of charge.

21.2 House of Timple- Casa Del Timple
In the centre of the former island capital **Teguise, the Casa Del Timple is** located diagonally opposite the church.

It is a palace built in the 18th century that has been converted into a museum. In three rooms, a collection of over 60 timepieces was assembled. Timples are small 5-sided musical instruments, comparable with guitars, on which traditional Canarian music was played and is still played at small concert events.

21.3 Museum of sacred art in Haría- Museo de Arte Sacro
The town of **Haría is** located in the north of the island and is nicknamed the Valley of a Thousand Palms.

Interesting is the **history of the church, which is** located in the center of the village. Through the wide avenue, planted with old laurel trees, one heads straight for the church.

From the outside it looks simple, like almost all churches on the island. Since one actually starts from an old masonry, it is astonishing that the interior does not fit in any way to the old sacral construction. The question arises why there is a church in this old village with an architectural style from the 1960s. The explanation can be found in the **Museo de Arte Sacro, on the** right next to the church, in an old manor house.

Old photos in the exhibition rooms show what happened: The old church, the **Iglesia de Nuestra Señora de la Encarnación**, was destroyed in a severe storm in 1956. Pictures in the first exhibition room document the fatal destruction.
In the other rooms of the manor house old relics are exhibited.

Admission is free. **Opening hours:** Tuesday, Thursday, Friday and Saturday from 10.00 - 15.00.
TIP: Combine your visit to the museum on Saturdays with the arts and crafts market, which takes place on the tree-lined avenue in front of the church.

21.4 Open Air Museum El Patio- Museo Agrícola El Patio

The agricultural museum **El Patio is located** at LZ-20 in Tiagua.

Dr. José Maria Barrete Fee (1924- 1993) founded the museum to preserve the ethnographic and cultural values of Lanzarote. The large complex essentially consists of 2 complexes. The ethnological museum is located in the former manor house from 1845. The topics that are described in German include: National geography, reflective texts, geology, pottery, architecture, folklore, traditional clothing, crafts and tourism.

One encounters old photographs, an exhibition of lava stones, pottery and chimney types.

At that time, the complex was the largest agricultural enterprise on the island, with 20 farmers working in agriculture with more than 15 camels. Interesting is the small house with inner courtyard with kitchen, bathroom, living room and bedroom, where the foreman of the estate lived until 1949. In the bedroom there are camp beds with straw mattresses on them, the carpets are made of woven palm branches.

The tour continues to a wine press, a bodega, a small cactus garden and a chapel.

Through the garden with typical island plants you reach an animal enclosure with a camel, goats, chickens and a windmill. This is followed by a second ethnological exhibition with paintings, ceramics, basketry, camel seats, carriages, handicrafts and everything that was needed for agriculture at the time. In the bodega white and red house wine, as well as Moscatel are offered to the sample.

Visit the beautifully maintained complex, with its farm atmosphere, where you will be transported back to the last century. From the upper fields you can see Famara and the island of La Graciosa.
Opening hours: 10.00 - 17.00, closed on Sundays.

21.5 Aviation Museum- Museo Aeronautico
The **aviation museum is located** directly at the airport. Follow the signs to **MUSEO and** you will immediately find yourself in front of the old airport terminal.

The airport building was used from 1946 to 1970. For those times it was the highlight of the island, but it was not prepared for the tourist rush of the 1970's, so that today's airport was built.
Impressive is how small the beginnings were on Lanzarote. On request, the museum staff will guide you through the rooms with additional explanatory descriptions.

In the first room there is a large picture with a picture from the 1930s showing Count Zeppelin over Las Palmas in Gran Canaria.

Other photographs show the beginnings of aviation and a landing in the bay of Arrecife in 1924.

In the adjoining room there is the former waiting room.
On the right is a reproduction of the long mural designed by César Manrique for the airport in 1953. It presents the island from north to south and contains many motives with recognition value as for example the rock of Famara, the volcano la Corona, the wine-growing area La Geria, typical houses, camels and the fire mountains up to Playa Blanca. The original is currently owned by Fundación César Manrique.
The purchase of the painting was documented on a sheet of paper in the typewriter on display. In 1953 the cost of the mural was 10,817.00 pesetas.
To the left of it, in the small room that is currently used for film screenings, was the souvenir shop.

In the back area, on the right side were the ticket counter, a small bar and the premises.

A large photo behind the bar, in which the original floor is still preserved, brings the VIPs of that era to life. From right to left, you can see Camilo Pajuelo Arteaga, the then head of the Civil Guard, Thomás Lamamié de Clairc, the delegate of the Iberia airline, Antonio Diaz Carrasco, the airport manager and Benjamin Madero, the chief physician of the Arrecife battalion.

To the left of the bar the passengers went to the exit. Before departure they had to stand individually with their luggage on the big scales to determine the weight for the airplane.

On the left side was the office of the airport director, which today is a small library with additional information on aviation.

In the front part of the building, a narrow staircase leads up to the upper floor of the control tower. Only a radio, a telephone, a clock, a pen and a book were sufficient to coordinate the flights. From the front you have a view of Terminal 2 of today's airport.

Opening hours: Mon - Sat from 10.00 - 14.00, free admission.

21.6 Wine Museum El Grifo- Museo El Grifo
The **Museum EL Grifo is located** in the wine-growing area of La Gería in the southwest of the island. On the LZ-30 road, which runs through the entire area, one bodega follows the other.

El Grifo is the oldest winery in the Canary Islands and one of the ten oldest in Spain. For over 2 centuries it was owned by two families, 5 generations of which were in the hands of the current owner family. The museum is located in the old winery, where there are historical tools for wine making from the 19th and early 20th centuries.
4 different grape varieties are cultivated, which are harvested between June and September as follows: Malvasia, Listan Negro, Syrah and Moscatel.

After payment, a plan is handed out at the entrance, which leads through the premises of the museum.

Among others, the following exhibits will be exhibited:
- A lever and beam press,
- a winepress,
- different presses,
- the wine label designed by César Manrique for his favourite wine, Semidulce,
- a barrel maker, a winepress
- A library and a laboratory.

In the second building there is a large label exhibition. Next to the exhibition room is the manor house, which may not be entered.

In the rear part of the complex there is a vineyard, which has the special feature that the vines were planted in solidified lava depressions.

A small cactus garden forms the conclusion.
After the visit there is the possibility to taste the wine included in the entrance fee.
Opening hours: daily 10.30- 18.00 o'clock

21.7 Museum of History in Arrecife- Museo de Historia de Arrecife
The museum, the **Museo de Historia de Arrecife**, is located in the Castillo San Gabriel, on the small island Islote de Fermina, not far from the main shopping street Calle Castillo y Léon of Arrecife.

The castle can be reached via two bridges, the left one is called **Puente de las Bolas** and is a small drawbridge with two cannonballs on the pillars.
In the 16th century the castle was replaced by a stone fortress, which served to protect the port and the town.

A museum guide with explanations of the overview boards is handed out at the entrance.
TIP: Enjoy the unique view over the sea and the capital from the upper floor.
Opening hours: Mon - Fri 10.00 - 17.00 h, Sat 10.00 - 14.00 h, closed on Sundays, free admission.

21.8 Cochineal Museum
The museum is located near the cactus garden, on the LZ- 42, the main road that leads through Mala.
Already at the entrance cacti were planted, which are occupied with Cochinellen.
The Cochinelle is a scale insect which was used for the production of red natural colours in the 19th century. For this purpose, cacti were infected with the pest. However, the cultivation lost importance when the product could be chemically manufactured. In the meantime, the Cochinelle is experiencing a revival, so that old cactus plantations in Guatiza and Mala are being reforested and restored.

The museum shows in detail the processing of the cochineal, from planting and harvesting to the production of the final product. In the following shop you can try and buy the new Aloe Vera Liqueur as well as many Aloe Vera products.
Opening hours: Daily from 10.30- 17.00 o'clock. Admission is free.

22   Unique island artists
22.1 The last basket weaver of Haría
Shortly after the Casa/ Museo César Manrique in Haría, on the right side, there is the last **basketry of** the island.

Inconspicuously, in a garage with green doors and wicker baskets hung in front of them, Señor Eulogio Concepcíon Perdomo sits on a small, low chair and weaves baskets of different sizes. For this purpose, the 86-year-old cuts dried palm branches into thin long strips in order to weave them in the traditional way.

In former times his works were more in demand, so that he appeared personally on craftsman markets. Meanwhile, due to his old age, the sale only takes place in his workshop. According to his own information he needs half a day to weave a small basket. The processed palm branches are provided by the gardeners of the Casa/ Museo César Manrique.

22.2 Autentica Ceramica Canaria in Haría
Traditional clay works, which were already made by the natives of the Canary Islands, can be found in Calle Fajardo in Haría.
The artist moved from his small studio in Maguez, which could only have been called a garage, to Haría to make his handicrafts even more popular.

Señor Joachim Reyes Betancort makes the sound himself. He mixes volcanic soil with clay and kneads the mixture with his feet until a sufficient consistency is achieved.

As he shapes his creations, he squeezes out the remaining small stones to obtain a smooth surface.

The finished objects are dried for several days and burned by him in the public kiln in the village. The actual firing process takes two days. On the first day he lights a small fire and adds wood every two hours. The next day more wood will be added. During the last 5 hours of the firing process, the wood supply is increased again and the stove is closed. It takes three to five days until the work has cooled down and can be removed.

By the way: All clay works are made without a potter's wheel. Please note that the freelance artist has no fixed opening hours. He now also makes beautiful jewellery and watercolours.

Tip: Visit the artist on **Saturdays in** conjunction with the crafts market in Haría. At the end of the market you will find the church, which you can pass on your right and at the end of the small street you will find the artist's building.

22.3 The German potter Birgit Groth
The studio is located in Calle Los Morros, 15 in 35542 Arrieta.

The artist has lived on the island since 2007 and creates new individual works every day, which she lovingly implements. The clay and over 100 glazes are embarked from Germany and fired on the island in the neighbouring town of Mozaga.

Especially popular are their mouse cups, which are food safe and can be used like all creations for daily use.

A special position among her works is held by the **stones of concern, for which there is the** following story of the artist: "At that time there was a country in fantasies where everything was normal. The weather was changeable, the people had jobs, the children raved, like all children - so, a really normal country. Sure,

sometimes it rained at the wrong time or the fish didn't bite properly or the children didn't obey.
But in one thing, the people of this country were different from other people. No one complained, complained, or lamented. And if someone said something, then someone else replied: "**Tell that to your worry stone**".
Yes, they were quite happy people - not that they didn't have any problems, but one thing distinguished them from other people. Everyone had their own problem stone - and that's how it came:
In former times people were full of worries and problems and everyone told them to everyone who had worries again and it came more often to Widerworten and also to the quarrel. One felt overwhelmed to listen to the problems of the others even to one's own worries. People were often discontented and in a bad mood.

One fine day now a fisherman, filled with sorrow and anger, goes down to the beach. He collects a handful of stones and throws them as far as he can into the sea. But a short time later the waves throw them back to the beach and they trundle at his feet. Still angry, he lifts the first of the rolling back stones and with a sweeping movement he wants to throw it back into the sea. But suddenly he hears a voice: "Wait, you're not getting anywhere."
Astonished, the fisherman takes down his arm and notices that the stone in his hand speaks these words. With his eyes wide open, he stares at the stone. "I feel sorry for you", says the stone and looks at the man "and therefore I will help you and the people in your country".
He smiles a little, "I'm a worry stone. You can confide with all your needs and problems. I won't tell! You can tell me anything - I'm not contradicting you! All your worries remain closed in me - I will be silent."

Then the stone rolls its little forehead into folds and whispers so quietly that our fisherman has to hold the stone to his ear to understand even the last words. "I've told you everything now, and I'll never speak again. Believe me, your worries will not necessarily diminish

with me, but now you have me to talk and think about it in peace. Take all the stones around you and give them to the people in your country. You'll feel better."
I said it, I did it! And already after a short time the people became happier and more cheerful and when somebody got angry, then it was said: **Tell that to your worry stone...**

Opening hours: Thu. and Fr. from 11.00- 13.00 and 15.00- 18.00 o'clock.
Further exhibits can be found at: www.toepferei-lanzarote.de
Contact details: E-mail: ruespel@t-online.de
Phone: 0034 928 848640
Facebook: Lanzarote Pottery Arrieta
Instagram: rubiarrieta2007
By the way: The artist also creates creations on customer request.

22.4 The Jolateros - boats and souvenirs made of recycled sheet metal

The **Jolateros are located** on the main road, the Carretera Los Castillos, shortly after the Castillo San José, direction Arrecife- El Charco de San Ginés. On the right side of the road you can see a big windmill, on the left side there are small, colourful boats on black lava stones. From here you follow the promenade.

A few steps further you will find the open-air workshop.

The history of the Jolateros, the only and last Lanzarote boatbuilders to produce 1-man boats from scrap metal, dates back to the 1930s. At that time the fishermen drove with these small boats to their cutters, nowadays they are only used for summer races by children in the Charco San Ginés in Arrecife.
Señor Antonio presents the production of his boats in miniature form to his visitors full of joy and passion.

With a pair of scissors he cuts a strip from a tin can of olive oil, takes a pair of pliers, bends the sharp edges inwards and then knocks them flat on a wooden board.

Then he forms the boat shape with his thumb and fingers, takes an adhesive, spreads it on two small pieces of wood and sticks them to the ends of the boat to fix them.
To test the final seaworthiness of the small new work of art, he places it in a plastic bowl filled with water. The souvenir is ready for sale with an individual coat of paint.

This old Lanzarote boat building art is worth seeing. Here you can buy a very special souvenir. The small boats can also be purchased as key rings for a small price.

By the way: According to the current state of affairs it is not certain whether Señor Antonio is allowed to stay at this location permanently, as the current owner would like to add the property to another use. Currently, if you do not see the metal boats and do not find him, he exhibits his exhibits in the rear part of the Charco de San Ginés.

23   Selected Discovery Tours
23.1 Fascinating viewpoints
On Lanzarote there are **unique vantage points** from which you can enjoy fantastic views and beautiful photos in clear weather.
Mirador del Rio: From the café and the viewing platform, one has a view to the island La Graciosa. In **Guinate, at** the end of the village, one can once again enjoy a free look over La Graciosa. The pretty tile on the wall with the inscription "Dejate Llevar" translated means "Let us carry you".

Gran Hotel Arrecife City: On the 17th floor of the Grandhotel there is a public café, with views over Arrecife, Puerto del Carmen and Fuerteventura.

The church **Ermita de Las Nieves:** unique panorama over the whole island up to Fuerteventura.

Pirate Museum- **Museo de la Pirateria** in Teguise: Magnificent view over Teguise and the whole island to Fuerteventura.

Femés: In clear weather conditions, one has a view from the viewing terrace on Playa Blanca up to the white beaches of Corralejo on Fuerteventura, with the island Los Lobos in front of it. For photos like in the Caribbean, you should translate to **La Graciosa**.

By the way: Unfortunately on Lanzarote you can never say when it is the best time to take beautiful photos. Spring and autumn are the best seasons to take photos from viewpoints. However, the weather can be unsettled even in these months. Strong winds can occur all year round and blow away the clouds after a few hours, resulting in a bright blue sky. But, at "Kalima" on Lanzarote one speaks of a hazy weather that brings dusty and sandy winds from Africa to the island.

In the summer months it is mostly cloudy until midday and there is often a light drizzle, but it lasts only for a short time. The landscape is accordingly kept in monotonous brown tones. After lush but short rains in the late autumn months, Lanzarote shines in a lush green with flowers.

23.2 The Northwest

The tour starts in the geographical centre of the island in **San Bartolomé**, at the **Monumento al Campesino**.

One drives towards Tinajo, through the villages Mozaga, Tao and Tiagua. In Tiagua there is the possibility to visit the **Museo Agricola El Patio.**

From Tinajo, continue towards **La Santa**, where the sports and leisure club of the same name is located.

On the way back, you drive via El Cuchillo and Soo to Caleta de **Famara**, a fishing village where you can watch surfers on the beach and enjoy a beautiful view of the island of **La Graciosa**.

You can also visit the **former island capital Teguise, which** captivates with its picturesque old town and has a 500-year history. The **Castillo Santa Barbara is** located on the volcanic mountain above Teguise, from where one has a wonderful view over the whole island.

23.3 The contrasting north

The northern tour, towards Órzola, starts in **Tahiche, where** the **Fundación César Manrique, the** famous house with underground lava bubbles, is located. From here take the LZ-1 towards Orzola. In Mala you can visit the new **Cochinella Museum**, in Guatiza you can visit the cactus garden, the **Jardín de Cactus.**

The path leads through the towns of Mala and Arrieta in the direction of Orzola- Jameos del Agua. Here one has the possibility to visit the **Jameos del Agua**, the cave with the small white albino crabs, as well as the **Cuevas de los Verdes, which are** located a little further above.

The journey continues along the coast through the **Malpais de La Corona**, the green heart of Lanzarote. The road leads past beautiful bays, the last of which, **Caleton Blanco, is** one of the most beautiful on the island.

23.4 The volcanic fiery center

This tour starts in the geographical centre of the island in **San Bartolomé**, at the **Monumento al Campesino, where** the **Farmers' Museum is** located.

From here we head towards **Masdache**, with the destination **La Geria**, the unique area characterized by its traditional viticulture.

The road ends in Uga, from where you drive towards Yaiza with a destination in the National Park, the Parque Nacional de **Timanfaya.**
Passing **Echadero de Camellos, with the** possibility of a camel ride, the road leads directly to the national park.

On the way to **Tinajo, there is the** Visitor Centre, the **Centro de Visitantes**, with audiovisual presentations and a footbridge leading into the rugged volcanic landscape of the Timanfaya region.
From here you can head for **Mancha Blanca** with the **Ermita de Los Dolores, the** patron saint of the island. Finally, in the direction of La Geria, at the end of the

road that runs through the beautiful volcanic landscape, you come back to the north in the direction of Monumento al Campesino, or to the south in the direction of La Geria.

23.5 The south coast
Take the southern road towards Yaiza, the village of the same name, which is characterised by its white and well-kept architecture.
From here you can head for the unique coastal ensemble: The **Salinas de Janubio**, **Los Hervideros**, **El Lago de los Clicos** and the fishing village **El Golfo**.

In the extreme south is **Playa Blanca**, with the famous **Papagayo beaches**.

On the way back, one drives over **Femes in** order to enjoy a beautiful view over the south of the island up to Fuerteventura. The route continues via **Las Casitas de Fémes**, back to the main axis, LZ-2, which runs in all directions.

23.6 Hike Montaña Colorada
At the LZ- 56 direction Timanfaya, after a short drive there are 2 stone walls on both sides with the inscription Municipio de Tinajo. Follow the road in the direction of Timanfaya.

For orientation, the Montaña Colorada is the second volcano on the right side of the road. At the roadside there is a small white-green sign with the inscription LZ-56 KM 4. Shortly after a stationary radar station, a bend and a no overtaking sign follow. Immediately afterwards you can turn right from the road onto Ascheplatz and park.
Now the border can start, a beautiful walk of 45 minutes through an impressive landscape. The degree of difficulty is low, as the path runs almost flat around the volcano cone. There are boards at 15 interesting points offering additional information in German.

After a short time one discovers why the volcano bears its name.

A red-hot volcanic landscape that one would not have expected from the previous page.

There is a **monolith** here that flew 20 km to this place during the eruptions of Timanfaya.

By the way: The sparkling **olive stones can be** found directly in the large field in front of the parking lot. It is not expressly forbidden to take stones with you, but you should leave it with smaller specimens and pack them in your suitcase and not in your hand luggage.

23.7 Hike Montaña del Cuervo
The **Montaña del Cuervo is located** at LZ- 56, direction Timanfaya National Park. After a short drive 2 lava stone walls with the inscription **Municipio de Tinajo** follow. Shortly after, on the right and left side, on smoothed ash pitches, you will find the parking facilities. Now you follow the beaten path, which is marked with stones at the edges.

The way will be documented in German language after about 10 minutes of walking by National Park operators.

A beautiful walk follows through a fascinating landscape to the volcano and into the crater.

From the crater, there is now the possibility to go back to the parking lot on the right, or to walk to the left to circumnavigate the volcano.

The mini-hike takes about 1,5 hours, if you walk around the volcano. Easy level of difficulty, but you should wear closed shoes, as the path is partly gravel-like.
Tip: Combine this hike with the Montaña Colorada, which is almost across the street, within reach.

23.8 Volcano Monte Corona - view into the crater

To the north is the highest volcano, **Monte Corona**, at 609 metres. Take a look inside the crater and take extraordinary photos.

The path is not signposted. It starts in the small village **Ye** and is located at LZ-10 between Guinate and the Mirador del Río, more precisely between church and restaurant, next to the house with the number 18.

The easiest way is to park in front of the small church and take the road towards Mirador del Río on foot. After the first house on the right side there is a large vineyard. The road becomes wider on the right side, the road marking is dotted here. Now you see a yellow and white road sign with the inscription LZ-201 KM 4, behind it there is a garbage container. Directly behind the field on the right, the path begins.

It leads past semicircular stone walls in which wine is planted in the middle, metal rods with empty plastic bottles hanging from their tips, feral stone walls, further and further up to the crater. The further up you get, the more rocky the path becomes. The ascent takes about 30 minutes, the return journey takes just as long.

For directional orientation you can hold on to the big palm tree.

One enjoys a wonderful view over the coast and opposite in the distance the Mirador del Río that is recognizable by the queues of cars parked in front of it.

Recommendation: Wear sturdy shoes as the upper part of the path is very rocky.

23.9 Tramelan Hike - The Hike through the National Park

There are still misinformations that one can simply drive to the Centro de Visitantes, the visitor centre in Mancha Blanca, in order to hike through the national park.

I inquired at the Centre's office and was informed that all the major guides had only written a question concerning the itinerary of the walk, which was answered. In non-updated records this information is no longer correct as it was provided before 1996.

I had decided to take the Tremesana route in Spanish because there was exactly one place left. The English tour was already fully booked.
When I arrived at the center, after a short time the names of the participants were called up and you had to enter your name, date of birth and passport number in a list and sign it, so I think it was in Spanish that you are physically fit.

Since my name can't be German as German, the guide asked me when he called "Müller" and I sat down to see if I could speak Spanish at all. After 10 sets and some jokes it was clear that my Spanish was sufficient from his point of view.
And then it started. I entered with my guide, a friendly sympathetic woman and the group, we were 8 people, into the jeep which was parked in front of the center. The English-speaking group sat next to it in the 2nd jeep.

We drove towards Timanfaya, past the camels, destination Yaiza. Already at the departure the travel guide reports in detail about the history of Lanzarote and the volcanic eruptions. When we arrived in Yaiza, we followed a bumpy path until we reached a barrier that opened it to enter the national park. The jeep was parked and our hike began.

Super interesting and informative, half way we met the English guided group.
One could ask questions, the group stopped at particularly interesting places and the travel guide revealed a knowledge that I had not heard before.
Thus, among other things, a huge monolith that is located next to the **Montaña Colorada**, where I had already been several times, was thrown 20 km far.

What I also didn't know until now is that it is not allowed to walk thoughtlessly over the ringed lava fields that are located, for example, in the area of the Monumento al Campesino, as the lava could have thrown bubbles underground and as soon as the lava layer is too thin, one could break in and injure oneself.

The excursion ended after about 2 hours at the height of El Golfo, where we got into the jeep of the other group and drove back to the center.

My conclusion: The Tremesana hike, which is carried out free of charge through the national park, is an absolute must for Lanzarote fans and who want to become one. A real experience!
Unfortunately, the tours are only offered in English and Spanish. For the Spanish leadership a fluent Spanish is assumed, a "Hola, que tal?" is not sufficient. In addition, it would be too unfortunate and unfair for the committed employees of the National Park to miss out on the information.
Important to know:
Visit the website of the National Park:
www.reservasparquesnacionales.es and select the route.
Reservations can only be made up to 2 months in advance, depending on occupancy. Age of participants: 16 years and older.

24 Cheese dairies- Queserías
On Lanzarote cheese production has a long tradition. The handmade goat cheese can be bought in the local cheese dairies and at weekly markets.
24.1 *Cheese dairy El Faro*
The **Queseria El Faro is** located in the north of the island, towards Teguise, on the LZ- 30. Parallel to the main road, behind a high wall, one discovers the countless goats that supply the milk for the cheese.
The courtyard of the company is kept very simple and in the tiny shop there is a manageable cheese counter.

Among the products on offer are fresh goat cheese, young, medieval and mature goat cheese, each in the varieties nature, paprika and gofio as well as smoked goat cheese.

In 2014, El Faro received the gold medal for its smoked goat's cheese at the official Canarian cheese dairy competition.
Opening hours: Mondays to Fridays: 10.00 - 14.00, Saturdays 8.00 - 13.00.

24.2 Rubicón Cheese Dairy
The **Queseria Rubicón is located in** Femés, in the south of the island. It is located below the small church of the village and is signposted at the roundabout.

We offer fresh goat cheese, matured, smoked goat cheese, as well as cheese with oregano, gofio and paprika powder. Next to the counter there is a selection of cheeses that can be tasted.

The **special feature of the** Rubicon cheese dairy: it is possible to have the cheese vacuum packed so that it can be taken to Germany. Daily fresh **goat milk** and **goat yoghurt are** offered. **By the way:** Opposite the cheese dairy there is a volcano mountain on which the house goats run around.

25   Bodega Los Almacenes/ Mama Trina
The **Bodega is located** at the LZ-1 direction Mirador del Río, in the north of the island. A few bends after the strikingly large yellow house on the left, a path leads directly to **Los Almacenes**.

In addition to wine and liqueurs, the sales room also offers the famous Mama Trina jams and mojo sauces for tasting and sale. Almost all products come from our own production.

The Bodega is open daily from 11.00 - 18.00 o'clock. The "Mama Trina" products, which are made according to old family recipes, are also available in many supermarkets and weekly markets.

Tip: Especially the jams and mojosauces are a great souvenir for those who stayed at home.

26   German Bakery Andy Bread - Panadería Andy Bread

The bakery is located in Tías, in calle Gabriel Diaz, 9. It is not immediately accessible as it is not clearly signposted. Coming from San Bartolomé you drive towards Tías, at the roundabout with the sign "Museo" straight on and immediately turn left on the first road. The small bakery is immediately on the right after the bend in which a garbage container stands.

The green door leads directly into the bakery. It smells deliciously delicious after fresh pastries, rolls and bread.

The special thing about bread is that it is made from wholemeal flour without baking agents and contains neither enzymes nor additives. For Andy bread, the dough is mixed with a 4-stage natural sourdough made from wholemeal rye flour. In alternately cool (strong taste) and later warm environment (yeast formation) the natural sourdough is given 48 hours time for fermentation. This makes it milder than dough produced more quickly (some sourdough only takes 3-5 hours to ripen) and much more tasty and digestible than "natural sourdough" made from artificial dough acidifiers, the so-called "artificial sourdoughs". Then wholemeal flour, water and a little salt are added and the dough is prepared, which rests again for several hours. Since the founding of the company in 2003, a residual quantity has been purchased as the basis for the next sourdough.
are offered: Whole grain rye bread (oat flakes), whole grain rye bread, whole grain rye nut bread, whole grain spelt bread (additionally with sunflower or pumpkin seeds), farmhouse bread (also with sunflower or pumpkin seeds), large grain rye nut bread, large farmhouse bread, gluten-free bread, box white bread, white baguette, Grain baguette, surprise baguette, ciabatta, bread roll selection, grain roll, wholemeal spelt roll, lye roll, lye pretzel, croissant, chocolate croissant, ham cheese croissant, raisin snail, raisin roll, muesli stick, yeast plait and cake in the varieties cherry, apple, plum, cheese and onion. **Opening hours:** Fridays and Saturdays from 7.00 am to 12.00 pm.

27   Aloe vera
Aloe vera is an ancient medicinal plant known for its healing properties and is found in cosmetic and pharmaceutical products.

The largest **Aloe Vera Museum is located** in Punta Mujeres.

The museum offers information boards about the history of the Aloe Vera plant, as well as its cultivation and use. In two further niches you can learn more about salt extraction on Lanzarote and the former shield lice breeding.

Friendly employees provide detailed information on the products and application areas.

Product information at: www.aloepluslanzarote.com

28   Aquarium- Costa Teguise
The **aquarium is located** in the Avenida Las Acacias, in Costa Teguise in the Centro Comercial El Trébol.

Through the souvenir shop after the payment it goes down into the underwater world.
The tour with its 33 aquariums is divided into 3 themes: Canary coasts, tropical reefs and open sea. In the aquariums of different sizes you can find the following sea creatures: bream, sea urchins, large tiger fish, mussels, snails, starfish, koi, moray eels, crabs, giltheads, sea urchins, lobsters, octopuses, rays, cat sharks, "Finds Nemo", fish camouflaged in the sand, anemones, spiny fish and small sharks.

When you walk through the small tunnel of the aquarium, the sharks are close to grab.
The Aquarium Lanzarote takes part in the program for the preservation and protection of the Caretta turtles, supported by the municipal office for environmental protection. The aim of the project is to preserve the species of these turtles, which are threatened with extinction. The turtles in the aquarium were found

seriously injured in the sea. After life-saving operations and healing of all injuries, these animals were admitted to our installations in order to provide them with a species-appropriate rehabilitation and then to reintegrate them into their natural environment, the open sea. Only the animals that could no longer survive in the open sea due to severe injuries remain in the aquarium."

Conclusion: Worth seeing for aquarium fans and children. The tour ends in a maximum of 35 minutes and you are at the exit, which leads upstairs to the souvenir shop.

29   Aquapark Costa Teguise
The water park is located in the Avenida Golf Parc 315, in Costa Teguise.

At the entrance there is a map with all attractions.

The Aquapark is open from mid-March to mid-November. From Costa Teguise it can be reached on foot or by taxi. It also offers a shuttle service to and from Puerto del Carmen and Playa Blanca for a fee.

Further information is available at: www.aquaparklanzarote.es
Note: The amusement park is getting on in years. In the high season it is more than difficult to find a couch, on the slides you have to show stamina. Child friendly, but extras such as driving electric cars have to be paid for.
By the way: The slides are no longer permitted if the body weight exceeds 100 kg.

30   Aqualava Playa Blanca
The small **water park Acualava is located in the** Calle Gran Canaria S/N, in Playa Blanca. It is open all year round and offers with 5 water slides, a current channel, a wave pool, a children's play area and a restaurant, the possibility to spend a nice day.

In addition to day tickets, 1- and 2 week tickets are offered at reasonable prices. More information at: www.aqualava.net

31   Hop On- Hop Off Arrecife
In order to get a small overview of the island capital Arrecife and the closer surroundings, one gets in and out of the Bimmelbahn with the Hop On- Hop Off principle as often as one likes.

City Sightseeing Arrecife offers 2 tours which can be used in one day with the ticket.
Red line: Charco San Ginés- Intercambiador de Guaguas, bus station- Gran Hotel Arrecife- Real Club Nautico- Castillo
San Gabriel - Marina Lanzarote, marina - Castillo San José

Blue line: Charco San Ginés- Castillo San José- Estacion de Guagas, bus station- Teatro insular, city theatre- Gran Hotel Arrecife- Real Club Nautico- Castillo San Gabriel- Marina Lanzarote.

Entry and exit can take place as often as you like, the fare is due once at the start of the journey. You will receive a city map and headphones that provide interesting and informative information about the tour's sights during the tour.
Start: 10.00 o'clock before the Castillo San Gabriel at the confluence of the main shopping street, Castillo Leon y Castillo. Last trip: 16.00.
The price for adults is 10,00 €, for children from 7-12 years 6,00 €, from 3-7 years 4,00 €. The fare includes admission to the Castillo San José.

32   Boat trip Puerto del Carmen - Puerto Calero
Lineas Romero offers a boat trip with the Express Waterbus from **Puerto del Carmen** to **Puerto Calero,** or vice versa, from Puerto Calero to Puerto del Carmen.
Tickets are available in the old port of Puerto del Carmen, directly in the office of Lineas Romero or at the end of the port of Puerto Calero, in the ticket shop.

It is possible to sit down below deck or enjoy the view on deck in the sun. From Puerto del Carmen: The boat travels along the coast and after 10 minutes of sailing time throttles the speed, so that one can observe the seabed through the glass bulkheads in the bottom of the ship for a few minutes.

Once you arrive in Puerto Calero, you can get off the boat, visit the port, have a bite to eat or drink, or stay on board and return.
Departure times Puerto Calero- Puerto del Carmen: 10.00, 11.15, 12.45, 14.15, 15.45 hrs.
Departure times Puerto del Carmen - Puerto Calero: 10.30, 12.00, 13.30, 15.00, 16.30 hrs.

Recommendation: Especially those who have not yet taken a water taxi will enjoy this little trip. Also recommendable for those who do not know the coast between Puerto del Carmen and Puerto Calero yet. Unfortunately, the trip is not recommended for people who get seasick quickly, as the ship wobbles slightly when leaving the harbours.

33   Pardelas Park- Pardelas Restaurant
The **Pardelas Park is** located in the north of Lanzarote. In Orzola follow the signs for **Granja Recereativa Zoo** and after about 1 km you will see the park on your right.

It's a little petting zoo. At the cash desk you get a bucket to feed rabbits, chickens and cocks, peacocks, ducks and chicks, pot-bellied pigs, ponies, horses, donkeys and goats.
It is fascinating to see how well the animals knew the buckets. As soon as you put the bucket on the ground, the ducks help themselves, the horses and the donkey scratch their hooves and the goats jump at you if you don't feed them immediately.

In the complex there is a large playground with slides and swings, children have the possibility to ride on a donkey and pottery.

The Las Pardelas restaurant is part of the complex, with Swiss chef Viktor Spillmann assuming responsibility for the Canarian cuisine since 2012.

Conclusion: The Pardelas Park is particularly suitable for parents with small children.

34   Rancho Texas Park

Rancho Texas Park is located on the LZ-40 expressway in **Puerto del Carmen**.

It is a combination of a zoo with an amusement park and a small aguapark. At the cash desk you get a plan, which leads you through the well-kept complex.

Among the new attractions are the penguins and the dolphin show.
On the picturesque route through the park, one can observe all the animals without having the feeling that they are imprisoned, as they are also partly behind glass panes.

There are 5 different shows in the park:
10.45 a.m.: Parrots - 1st performance
11.30 a.m.: Dolphin 1st performance
12.10 am: Lasso show - only performance
12.30 p.m.: Sea lions - 1st performance
1:00 p.m.: Eagle 1st performance
1.30 pm: Parrots - 2nd performance
1.45 p.m.: Dolphin 2nd performance
2.30 p.m.: Sea lions - 2nd performance
15.00 h: Eagle- 2nd performance
16.00 o'clock: Parrots - 3rd presentation

In the middle part of the area there is a fast food restaurant that is designed like a huge western saloon. This is where the lasso show takes place.
The water park invites you to sunbathe and bathe afterwards.
Family: Especially parents with children will get their money's worth. For the kids there are playgrounds, play zones, western carriages, pony rides and a large adventure pool in the Aguapark.

It is reassuring to know that both the cats of prey that come from circus captivity and the penguins from the now closed Guinate Zoo can spend their old age here.
Opening hours: 9.30- 17.30 o'clock

Info: The journey can also be made with shuttle buses from Puerto del Carmen free of charge and from Costa Teguise and Playa Blanca.
Further information is available at:
www.ranchtexaslanzarote.com

35 Bodega La Querencia
The Bodega is located in the wine-growing area of La Geria on LZ-30. Coming from San Bartolomé, it is the first winery on the left before the Bodega Rubicon. At the road signs with the inscription **Vino- Wine point to the** access road to the winery.

The owner, Mr. Luciano, who unfortunately only speaks Spanish, told me that his family is growing wine in the 5th generation. On its 30,000 square meters, it produces between 7 and 8000 liters annually. When I asked him how the name of the bodega came about, he told me that he had 4 other brothers who claimed the land after his father's death.

Everybody said "yo quiero", "I want". So he paid off his brothers and was the new owner of this vineyard.
Mr. Luciano showed me how he produces the wine. In the left part of the bogega there is a brick corner, where the grapes are stomped with their feet and then put into the wine press. The juice is then pressed.

He produces Malvasia, Listán blanco and negro, as well as Moscatel.
After a short tasting I decided for a Listán negro, which was bottled and corked before my eyes.

My conclusion: A small, privately run bodega where there is no mass crowd. The owners' house is directly connected to the bodega.
I tried tapas here. You could choose between goat cheese, tomatoes or Ropa vieja.

36   Telamon- The Titanic of Las Caletas Bay
On 21.10.1981 the Greek cargo ship **Telamon** left San Pedro on the African Ivory Coast to set course for the port city of Thessaloniki, which was to be supplied with tree trunks and fuel.

When the freighter was almost 6 weeks later, on 31.10.1981 in the strait La Bocaina, between Lanzarote and Fuerteventura, an enormous storm caused extreme damage to the cargo hold of the then almost 30-year-old ship.

The captain declared a state of emergency and the freighter was manoeuvred to the shore of Las Caletas Bay in order not to block the port of Los Marmoles.
The logs were not given any further attention at the time, but 260 tonnes of heavy oil and 60 tonnes of diesel had to be carefully pumped out to prevent an oil disaster.
Since the Greek owner gave up his cargo ship, another interested party decided against repairing and transporting the Telamon due to the estimated costs of 100 million pesetas, today approx. 600,000 €, the Telamon remained there until today.
During a later storm the freighter broke into 2 parts, so that only the part above the water surface can be seen.

The Telamon was the big attraction of the Lanzaroteños because of its size, but it has turned into a ruin that became dangerous for bathers and divers.

José Torres, President of the Chamber of Commerce, was the first to sound the alarm and send a letter to the Port Authority pointing out the fatal condition of the freighter.

In 2009 Telamon attracted media attention for the last time. It was the cargo of the ship. The tree trunks, which lay on land for almost 30 years, were exposed to the weather there and only barely escaped destruction by fire, were staged by the Spanish city planner José Maria Pérez Sánchez as a large sculpture in the roundabout at Las Cucharas Beach in Costa Teguise. After a storm in September 2016, the sculpture was removed without replacement. In addition, in the same month a diving and camping ban was imposed on the section around Telamon, which continues to this day.

37 Rental car
Explore the island simply and relaxed with a rental car. Both the rental and the petrol prices are more than favourable. The largest provider on the island is Cabrera Medina- CICAR, followed by PLUSCAR.

Both companies are very strongly represented in the holiday regions with branches, so that you can decide for a rental car directly on the spot. In addition, rental cars can also be hired from smaller, private providers.

Tip: Visit the websites of the car rental companies to compare all offers.

38 Anti- Boredom Activities
Have you been bored and visited everything worth seeing? Even if Lanzarote seems to be rather small, there are more possibilities here than one would guess. From water sports to safaris and hikes to visiting the casino, there are countless alternatives to the pool. In order to get an overview of the whole programme, it is best to visit a tourist information office that is located in every holiday resort.

All current flyers are available here and on request you will be informed about current festivals and events.

39   Lanzarote with children
Particularly recommendable:
- Hop- on Hop- Off- Sightseeing with the Bimmelbahn
- Rancho Texas Park Animals and Bathing
- Airport Museum- Nostalgia
- Pardelas park petting zoo
- Caleton Blanco - sunbathing and bathing
- Waterparks- Costa Teguise and Playa Blanca
- Bauerndorf- Creative Workshops
- Aquarium- "Finding Nemo" to look at

Printed in Great Britain
by Amazon

ISBN 9781090932402